"In *Behold and Believe*, Courtney Doctor and Joanna Kimbrel have put together a study that helps us immerse ourselves in the fullness of all that Jesus meant in his 'I am' statements so that we can not only understand them but also find in them more reasons to love him."

Nancy Guthrie, author; Bible teacher

"If we become what we behold, there's no better focus for our gaze than Christ himself! *Behold and Believe* is a helpful resource for anyone who wants to understand (or remember anew!) who Jesus really is."

Ruth Chou Simons, *Wall Street Journal* bestselling author; artist; Founder, GraceLaced.com

"We often go to Scripture looking for ourselves, but we will better understand who we are and how we are to live when we have first looked long at Jesus. *Behold and Believe* lifts our gaze to Christ with deep, thoughtful study that helps us see that all of Scripture points to a Savior who is exactly who he said he was."

Glenna Marshall, author, *The Promise Is His Presence*; *Everyday Faithfulness*; and *Memorizing Scripture*

"Do you need an invitation to come and sit under the word and hear Jesus introduce himself to you? This study is just that! It's filled with rich truth wrapped in a helpful format that will cause you to see the Lord more clearly. To behold him with this kind of clarity is to believe that he is exactly who he says he is. I highly recommend this study!"

Vanessa K. Hawkins, Director of Community Life, Redeemer Lincoln Square, New York City

"This seven-week Bible study is true nourishment for the soul. Each week and each "I am" statement of Jesus allows the reader to know her Savior better. This is a feast—whether you're seeing Jesus for the first time or have known him for most of your life. I cannot wait to do this study with the women from my local church."

Jen Oshman, author, *Enough about Me* and *Cultural Counterfeits*; Women's Ministry Coordinator, Redemption Parker, Colorado

Behold and Believe

Behold and Believe

A Bible Study on the "I Am" Statements of Jesus

Courtney Doctor and Joanna Kimbrel

CROSSWAY®

WHEATON, ILLINOIS

Behold and Believe: A Bible Study on the "I Am" Statements of Jesus
Copyright © 2024 by Courtney Doctor and Joanna Kimbrel
Published by Crossway
          1300 Crescent Street
          Wheaton, Illinois 60187

Cover design: Dan Farrell

Cover image: Erin Spencer, erinspencerart.com

First printing 2024

Printed in China

All emphases in Scripture quotations have been added by the authors.

Trade paperback ISBN: 978-1-4335-9019-1
ePub ISBN: 978-1-4335-9022-1
PDF ISBN: 978-1-4335-9020-7

Library of Congress Cataloging-in-Publication Data
Names: Doctor, Courtney, 1967– author. | Kimbrel, Joanna, 1991– author.
Title: Behold and believe : a Bible study on the I am statements of Jesus / Courtney Doctor and Joanna Kimbrel.
Description: Wheaton, Illinois : Crossway, 2024. | Series: The gospel coalition | Includes bibliographical references.
Identifiers: LCCN 2023010313 (print) | LCCN 2023010314 (ebook) | ISBN 9781433590191 (trade paperback) | ISBN 9781433590207 (pdf) | ISBN 9781433590221 (epub)
Subjects: LCSH: Jesus Christ—Divinity—Sermons. | God (Christianity)—Name—Sermons. | Bible—Study and teaching. | Christian women—Religious life.
Classification: LCC BT216.3 .D63 2024 (print) | LCC BT216.3 (ebook) | DDC 226.5/06—dc23/eng/20230623
LC record available at https://lccn.loc.gov/2023010313
LC ebook record available at https://lccn.loc.gov/2023010314

Crossway is a publishing ministry of Good News Publishers.

RRD			33	32	31	30	29	28	27	26	25	24
15	14	13	12	11	10	9	8	7	6	5	4	3	2	1

To Jules
My prayer for you is that you will see more and more of our beautiful Savior and that
your seeing will lead to deep belief all the days of your life. I love you, sweet girl.
CC

To Eliana, Grace, and Kaylee
May you behold the beauty of Jesus and believe in him.
Love, Mom

ABOUT THE COVER ARTWORK

The artwork featured on the cover of this study is an original painting by Erin Spencer (b. 1979), an accomplished impressionist landscape artist whose work has been exhibited and included in private collections around the world.

Despite its overall sense of tranquility, this work contains representations of all seven of the "I Am" statements of Jesus. The sheep on the hillside convey "I am the good shepherd." The doorway conveys "I am the door." The pathway leading the viewer in conveys "I am the way, the truth, and the life." The vineyards in the lower left convey "I am the true vine." The wheat field in the lower right conveys "I am the bread of life." And lastly, the soft, warm light and emerging sunrise convey "I am the light of the world" and "I am the resurrection and the life."

Contents

Introduction

I grew up in the Midwest and lived in Colorado for several years. As a result, I'm quite used to snow. However, when we moved to Mississippi, I figured that snow-filled winters were a thing of the past. But I was wrong. One January day, the flakes began to fall. Big, fluffy, white flakes of snow. And while I was excited to see my beloved snow, I was not prepared for the reaction of those around me.

I was working in a hospital, and as the news began to spread that it was snowing, everyone began running to the windows to see. Nurses and doctors barged into patients' rooms, not to check on their patients, but to see the snow. In the hallways I could hear people—patients, families of patients, hospital staff, medical providers—saying to whomever was around, "Come and see—you won't believe it!" What they meant was, for someone to believe it was snowing, that person was going to have to see it with her own eyes. Because, for most of us, seeing is believing.

Later that day, I called my parents to tell them about the snow. Do you think they believed me? Of course they did! Even though they had not been able to see it snow in Mississippi with their own eyes, they believed me because I had seen it with mine.

When we see something amazing, we want to tell others. This is what John was doing for us when he wrote his Gospel. He was an eyewitness to all he recorded. John was not only one of the twelve disciples, but he was also the one referred to as the "disciple whom Jesus loved" (John 21:7, 20). And John wants his readers to behold Jesus. He wants us to see what Jesus did and who Jesus is. But more than just seeing Jesus, he wants us to believe in him.

John used the word "believe" at least fifty-four times in his Gospel. He began by telling us what John the Baptist's role was. "He [John the Baptist] came as a witness, to bear witness about the light, *that all might believe through him*" (1:7). John told us that his reason for writing his Gospel account was to testify to what he saw with his own eyes so that we would believe: "He who saw it has borne witness—his testimony is true, and he knows that he is telling the truth—that you also may believe" (19:35). And John ended his Gospel by saying that Jesus did a lot more than just what had been written down: "These are written so that you may believe that Jesus is the Christ, the Son of God, and that by believing you may have life in his name" (20:31).

I think John knew that seeing is believing, so he invites us to see Jesus through his own eyewitness account. Early in John's Gospel we read what John the Baptist said when he first saw Jesus: "Behold, the Lamb of God, who takes away the sin of the world!" (1:29). Martha testified, "I believe that you are the Christ, the Son of God, who is coming into the world" (11:27). Later we read what Pontius Pilate said about Jesus: "Behold your King!" (19:14).

Jesus is most certainly the Lamb of God who died for us, the Son of God who came for us, and the King of all kings who reigns over all things. However, in this study we are going to focus on what Jesus said about himself. Because more than what other people said about him, John gives us a front-row seat to what Jesus said. We will see that Jesus boldly and clearly proclaimed that he is the bread of life; the light of the world; the door of the sheep; the good shepherd; the resurrection and the life; the way, the truth, the life; and the true vine. He invites us to come and see.

So whether you are a Christian who needs to behold Jesus again and again or someone who is curious about Jesus and wants to explore Christianity, join me as we behold Jesus. Join me in looking long and hard at who Jesus said he is. And may our beholding lead to believing—because by believing we will live.

How to Use This Study

In this study, we want to glean important truths from God's word while also learning and applying trustworthy Bible study techniques. We'll do this by observing, interpreting, and applying each passage of Scripture over the course of five days of study.

Day 1 will always be observation—reading the passage and asking the question *What does the text say*? In this study, we'll hear from Jesus himself as he tells us who he is in the Gospel of John. Day 1 will involve slowly reading the passage several times while paying attention to details like repeated words and main ideas. You may have questions as you read. It's okay not to have all the answers or even to be a bit confused as you read certain passages. Write your questions in the margins and see if you can answer them by the end of the week.

Day 2 will focus on interpretation. We'll read the passage again and ask, *What does the text mean*? We'll focus on details like figurative language, argument, and context of the passage as we begin to interpret it.

Day 3 will continue to concentrate on interpretation by asking, *What does the whole Bible say*? We'll read other relevant and related passages in Scripture and ask the question *How does the rest of Scripture help me understand this text*?

Day 4 will focus on application. Once we've come to an understanding of the text's meaning, we'll ask the question *How can I faithfully respond*? As we pay attention to what Jesus teaches us, we'll consider what he shows us about himself, what he calls us to believe, and how we should live in response. God's word transforms how we think, what we love, and what we do. Time with Jesus changes us from the inside out.

Each week will end on Day 5 with a reflection. After reading it, you'll have an opportunity to answer some more questions about what you've learned that week.

Plan on approximately 20 minutes of study each day (or 1.5 hours each week). Each day will begin with prayer—a time for you to ask God to meet you as you study his living and active word. We recommend that you have an actual Bible in front of you rather than using an app on your phone or computer. You'll need it for cross-referencing verses, and a physical copy helps you more readily see the passage in its context. The provided Bible passages are from the English Standard Version, but feel free to use whatever translation you prefer.

Memory Work

A memory verse(s) is provided each week. Spend a few minutes each day working on memorizing it. The discipline of hiding God's word in your heart is one that will bear much fruit in your own life and the lives of those around you.

Discussion Questions

At the end of each chapter, you'll find a list of questions for group discussion. These are based on the work you've done throughout the week. There is an "icebreaker" question and a "warm-up" question. Each is intended to be a quick, easy, and fun way to get the group going. Keep the answers to these short so you have plenty of time to dig into the text together.

Videos

We hope to provide videos of the keynote teaching sessions from TGCW24. Each video will align with the chapters and will, Lord willing, be available after the conference in June 2024 at https://www.thegospelcoalition.org/tgcw24.

May you experience abundant life and enduring joy as you encounter Jesus Christ—the way, the truth, and the life.

> These are written so that you may believe that Jesus is the Christ, the Son of God, and that by believing you may have life in his name. (John 20:31)

1

I Am the Bread of Life

Have you ever been to an event where everyone wore name tags? Whether a Christmas party, a Bible study, or a networking event, red stickers that said, "Hello, my name is . . ." decorated everyone's shirt. Name tags identify the people we're talking to. But maybe name tags would be more helpful if instead of saying, "Hi, my name is Maria" or "Hi, my name is Herb," they told us something about that person. Wouldn't you rather read, "Hi, I'm a neurosurgeon who loves tacos and dogs," or, "Hi, I'm a poli-sci student who loves to debate immigration reform"?

This week we'll study the first of Jesus's seven "I am" statements. These statements are like Jesus's name tag telling us exactly who he claims to be. In John's Gospel, Jesus taught about himself in two ways. He *declared* who he was through "I am" statements, and he *showed* who he was by performing miraculous signs. All his teaching and actions proclaimed to the watching world, *I am God!*

Our world has a lot of opinions and questions about Jesus. *Who was he really?* Perhaps he was simply a good moral teacher. Perhaps he was a servant of the people. Perhaps he was a wrongly accused man with loyal friends who wanted to see his conviction overturned. Perhaps Jesus was just a really wise and good person we should imitate. Maybe you grew up in church and know a lot about Jesus, or maybe you've never studied the Bible before and have a lot of questions about who Jesus is.

The best way to get to know people is to sit with them and let them tell you about themselves. These "I am" statements are an amazing opportunity to sit with Jesus and let him introduce himself to you. Whether you've known Jesus for years or are just starting to explore Christianity, I think you'll find that Jesus will surprise you.

This week we'll have an opportunity to learn about Jesus through a miraculous sign that's combined with his first "I am" statement. Miraculously, Jesus fed five thousand hungry people with one boy's lunch. After their mouths tasted the goodness, their ears heard the first of the "I am" statements, "I am the bread of life."

If you are new to thinking about Jesus (or even if you've known him for a long time), it could seem strange that the Son of God compares himself to food. Over the next few days we'll find out what Jesus meant and why it's good news for spiritually hungry people.

⬆ Prayer for the Week

Father God, show me yourself as you show me your Son. Give me wisdom to understand your word, and open my eyes to see wondrous things from it. Help me to see who Jesus is, to believe what is true, and to live transformed by your word. In Jesus's name, Amen.

💜 Memory Verse

"Jesus said to them, 'I am the bread of life; whoever comes to me shall not hunger, and whoever believes in me shall never thirst.'" *John 6:35*

OBSERVATION:
What Does the Text Say?

John 6:1-71

After this Jesus went away to the other side of the Sea of Galilee, which is the Sea of Tiberias. And a large crowd was following him, because they saw the signs that he was doing on the sick. Jesus went up on the mountain, and there he sat down with his disciples. Now the Passover, the feast of the Jews, was at hand. Lifting up his eyes, then, and seeing that a large crowd was coming toward him, Jesus said to Philip, "Where are we to buy bread, so that these people may eat?" He said this to test him, for he himself knew what he would do. Philip answered him, "Two hundred denarii worth of bread would not be enough for each of them to get a little." One of his disciples, Andrew, Simon Peter's brother, said to him, "There is a boy here who has five barley loaves and two fish, but what are they for so many?" Jesus said, "Have the people sit down." Now there was much grass in the place. So the men sat down, about five thousand in number. Jesus then took the loaves, and when he had given thanks, he distributed them to those who were seated. So also the fish, as much as they wanted. And when they had eaten their fill, he told his disciples, "Gather up the leftover fragments, that nothing may be lost." So they gathered them up and filled twelve baskets with fragments from the five barley loaves left by those who had eaten. When the people saw the sign that he had done, they said, "This is indeed the Prophet who is to come into the world!"

Perceiving then that they were about to come and take him by force to make him king, Jesus withdrew again to the mountain by himself.

When evening came, his disciples went down to the sea, got into a boat, and started across the sea to Capernaum. It was now dark, and Jesus had not yet come to them. The sea became rough because a strong wind was blowing. When they had rowed about three or four miles, they saw Jesus walking on the sea and coming near the boat, and they were frightened. But he said to them, "It is I; do not be afraid." Then they were glad to take him into the boat, and immediately the boat was at the land to which they were going.

On the next day the crowd that remained on the other side of the sea saw that there had been only one boat there, and that Jesus had not entered the boat with his disciples, but that his disciples had gone away alone. Other boats from Tiberias came near the place where they had eaten the bread after the Lord had given thanks. So when the crowd saw that Jesus was not there, nor his disciples, they themselves got into the boats and went to Capernaum, seeking Jesus.

When they found him on the other side of the sea, they said to him, "Rabbi, when did you come here?" Jesus answered them, "Truly, truly, I say to you, you are seeking me, not because you saw signs, but because you ate your fill of the loaves. Do not work for the food that perishes, but for the food that endures to eternal life, which the Son of Man will give to you. For on him God the Father has set his seal." Then they said to him, "What must we do, to be doing the works of God?" Jesus answered them, "This is the work of God, that you believe in him whom he has sent." So they said to him, "Then what sign do you do, that we may see and believe you? What work do you perform? Our fathers ate the manna in the wilderness; as it is written, 'He gave them bread from heaven to eat.'" Jesus then said to them, "Truly, truly, I say to you, it was not Moses who gave you the bread from heaven, but my Father gives you the true bread from heaven. For the bread of God is he who comes down from heaven and gives life to the world." They said to him, "Sir, give us this bread always."

Jesus said to them, "I am the bread of life; whoever comes to me shall not hunger, and whoever believes in me shall never thirst. But I said to you that you have seen me and yet do not believe. All that the Father gives me will come to me, and whoever comes to me I will never cast out. For I have come down from heaven, not to do my own will but the will of him who sent me. And this is the will of him who sent me, that I should lose nothing of all that he has given me, but raise it up on the last day. For this is the will of my Father, that everyone who looks on the Son and believes in him should have eternal life, and I will raise him up on the last day."

So the Jews grumbled about him, because he said, "I am the bread that came down from heaven." They said, "Is not this Jesus, the son of Joseph, whose father and mother we know? How does he now say, 'I have come down from heaven'?" Jesus answered them, "Do not grumble among yourselves. No one can come to me unless the Father who sent me draws him. And I will raise him up on the last day. It is written in the Prophets, 'And they will all be taught by God.' Everyone who has heard and learned from the Father comes to me—not that anyone has seen the Father except he who is from God; he has seen the Father. Truly, truly, I say to you, whoever believes has eternal life. I am the bread of life. Your fathers ate the manna in the wilderness, and they died. This is the bread that comes down from heaven, so that one may eat of it and not die. I am the living bread that came down from heaven. If anyone eats of this bread, he will live forever. And the bread that I will give for the life of the world is my flesh."

The Jews then disputed among themselves, saying, "How can this man give us his flesh to eat?" So Jesus said to them, "Truly, truly, I say to you, unless you eat the flesh of the Son of Man and drink his blood, you have no life in you. Whoever feeds on my flesh and drinks my blood has eternal life, and I will raise him up on the last day. For my flesh is true food, and my blood is true drink. Whoever feeds on my flesh and drinks my blood abides in me, and I in him. As the living Father sent me, and I live because of the Father, so whoever feeds on me, he also will live because of me. This is the bread that came down from heaven, not like the bread the fathers ate, and died. Whoever feeds on this bread will live forever." Jesus said these things in the synagogue, as he taught at Capernaum.

When many of his disciples heard it, they said, "This is a hard saying; who can listen to it?" But Jesus, knowing in himself that his disciples were grumbling about this, said to them, "Do you take offense at this? Then what if you were to see the Son of Man ascending to where he was before? It is the Spirit who gives life; the flesh is no help at all. The words that I have spoken to you are spirit and life. But there are some of you who do not believe." (For Jesus knew from the beginning who those were who did not believe, and who it was who would betray him.) And he said, "This is why I told you that no one can come to me unless it is granted him by the Father."

After this many of his disciples turned back and no longer walked with him. So Jesus said to the twelve, "Do you want to go away as well?" Simon Peter answered him, "Lord, to whom shall we go? You have the words of eternal life, and we have believed, and have come to know, that you are the Holy One of God." Jesus answered them, "Did I not choose you, the twelve? And yet one of you is a devil." He spoke of Judas the son of Simon Iscariot, for he, one of the twelve, was going to betray him.

———

Today we will observe what the text says. The goal of observation is to trace the storyline, ask good questions, and look for details that will help us understand the passage. Begin with prayer and then read all of John 6, paying special attention to verses 25–40.

1. This story has a variety of characters. Write down what you learn about each of them. Also, write down if you have any questions about the different characters.

The disciples:

_____

_____

Jesus:

_____

_____

God the Father:

_____

_____

Moses:

_____

_____

Joseph:

_____

_____

The Holy Spirit:

_____

_____

The prophets:

_____

_____

The Jews:

_____

_____

Simon Peter:

_____

_____

Judas:

_____

_____

2. How did the Jews respond to Jesus's teaching (vv. 41, 42, 52)? How did his own disciples respond (vv. 60–71)?

_____

_____

_____

_____

3. When a word or idea is repeated, it usually means it's important. Highlight or underline every reference to *life*, *eternal life*, and *living* in the text. How many references did you find? Did you notice any other repeated ideas in the text?

_____

_____

_____

_____

4. What did Jesus say is the work of God (v. 29)?

_____

_____

5. Jesus repeatedly invited his listeners to believe and follow him. What are the results of believing in Jesus, coming to Jesus, or following Jesus, according to each of the following verses?

v. 35

v. 36

v. 40

v. 44

v. 47

6. Just as the food we eat impacts our bodies, Jesus claimed that eating the bread of life impacts our lives. What are the results of consuming the bread of life, according to each of the following verses?

v. 50

_____

_____

v. 51

_____

_____

v. 54

_____

_____

v. 56

_____

_____

v. 57

_____

_____

v. 58

_____

_____

7. Did anything about Jesus or his interactions with others surprise you in this passage? What are some questions you have about the story?

_____

_____

After reading today's passage, you may feel like you have more questions than answers, and that's okay! Even many of his disciples struggled with his claims. Understanding the Bible takes time, and we'll go a little deeper every day. Keep thinking about Jesus's words as you go about your day—especially at mealtime! Jesus claimed to be better than any kind of food. As you eat your meals this week, reflect on the importance of food in your own life and what it means that Jesus offers everlasting nourishment to everyone who trusts in him.

🤍 Memory Verse:

"Jesus said to them, 'I am the bread of life; whoever comes to me shall not hunger, and whoever believes in me shall never thirst.'" _John 6:35_

INTERPRETATION:
What Does the Text Mean?

Yesterday we observed the details of the passage, and today we'll dig a little deeper into our understanding of what it means. Good interpretation flows from thoughtful observation, so read the passage again. Begin with prayer, asking God to give you wisdom as you study.

Read John 6.

How would you respond if someone told you, "I am the bread of life"? It's a bold claim, and many of us would dismiss it as arrogant or even delusional. But before Jesus claimed to be the bread of life, he gave us a reason to listen. Jesus performed a miraculous sign where he fed five thousand people with only five small loaves of bread and two fish (John 6:1–15). Now imagine sitting in that crowd and having your fill of the miracle bread Jesus provided. Maybe now his audacious claim is worth considering.

1. When Jesus claimed to be the bread of life, he used a metaphor to explain something about who he is and what he accomplishes. The metaphor has two primary elements: the bread of life, and the act of eating the bread. Use the verses below to help you determine what each of these elements represents.

   Bread (vv. 51–55):

   _____

   _____

   Eating the bread (vv. 35, 47):

   _____

   _____

2. The Bible often uses "bread" to refer to food in general. What different functions does food have in our lives? How might the "bread of life" metaphor reveal what Jesus provides for those who believe in him?

   _____

   _____

   _____

   _____

3. Jesus offered a solution for the problem of death. How were the people he addressed seeking to solve that problem? What are some ways people try to cope with that problem today? How is Jesus's solution different?

4. What kind of hunger and thirst do you think Jesus meant in verse 35? How do you see that kind of hunger and thirst in our world today?

5. What does Jesus's explanation of "the work of God" in verses 26–29 tell us about the way to receive eternal life? How does Jesus's answer to the question, "What must we do, to be doing the works of God?" reveal misunderstanding in those who asked it?

6. Jesus told the Jews that they saw him but still didn't believe (v. 36). What did the Jews believe about him that caused them to seek him out? What kind of belief does Jesus require, which they lacked? (See vv. 29, 40, 46–47, 51, 57)

_____

_____

_____

_____

7. Jesus promised life that is available now and life "on the last day." Look back at the references to life, eternal life, and living that you highlighted yesterday. How would you describe the differences between these two categories of life, based on what you can gather from the text?

_____

_____

_____

_____

We know what it's like to crave food that will satisfy our hunger and sustain us through the day. We need protein, fat, and carbohydrates to keep us alive, but more than that, we need spiritual food. What Jesus promised is so much greater than a free meal and a full stomach. To feast with faith on the bread of life by believing in Jesus is to receive life that lasts forever. Our bodies may die, but Jesus is the food that sustains our souls forever.

💚 Memory Verse

"Jesus said to them, 'I am the bread of life; whoever comes to me shall not hunger, and whoever believes in me shall never thirst.'" *John 6:35*

INTERPRETATION:
What Does the Whole Bible Say?

Today we'll continue our interpretation of the text by exploring what other parts of the Bible have to say about the topics in this passage. Other passages of Scripture can help us understand this story in deeper ways. Begin with prayer, asking God to give you wisdom to see how the whole Bible informs your understanding of John 6, then read John 6 again before answering the questions below.

All this talk about bread of life might be strange to us, but to the Jews Jesus addressed, it sounded a lot like what they grew up hearing in the book of Exodus. At the beginning of Exodus, God's people, the Israelites, had been enslaved in Egypt for about four hundred years. God raised up a man named Moses to deliver the Israelites from slavery. He brought them out of Egypt and led them into the wilderness to bring them to the promised land of Canaan. While they were in the wilderness, they became hungry, and God miraculously provided bread from heaven for them to eat. Read Exodus 16 and then answer the questions below.

1. In your own words, summarize what happened in Exodus 16.

_____

_____

_____

_____

Scripture frequently points to the exodus from Egypt as a central picture of God's salvation. The Jews knew Exodus 16 and likely understood that Jesus was claiming to offer salvation as God did then.

2. In John 6:32, Jesus said, "Truly, truly, I say to you, it was not Moses who gave you the bread from heaven, but my Father gives you the true bread from heaven." Fill out the chart below to show how Jesus is the bread of life that is better than the manna in the wilderness.

Manna in the Wilderness	Jesus as the Bread of Life
Example: The people couldn't keep the extra manna or it would spoil.	Example: v. 27. Jesus said he gives food that does not perish.
The Israelites grumbled at God about their hunger and later about the manna (see Num. 21:5).	v. 41
The manna left them hungry again.	v. 35
The Israelites ate the manna but still died.	v. 50

3. What would have happened to the Israelites if God hadn't provided manna? What was Jesus attempting to communicate to his listeners by comparing himself to the manna in the wilderness?

_____

_____

_____

_____

4. Deuteronomy 8:3 explains why God provided manna, saying, "He humbled you and let you hunger and fed you with manna, which you did not know, nor did your fathers know, that he might make you know that man does not live by bread alone, but man lives by every word that comes from the mouth of the LORD." What similarities do you see between this verse and Jesus's message in John 6?

In the Old Testament, God promised repeatedly to send a Messiah, and the New Testament tells us the Messiah is Jesus. Messiah means "anointed one," and God promised that his anointed one would bring salvation, life, and peace. Isaiah 55 is about the coming Messiah, and just like Jesus's words in John 6, the passage in Isaiah talks a lot about food! Read Isaiah 55:1–3, then answer the questions below.

* How do Jesus's words in John 6:35 fulfill this prophecy? What does that fulfillment tell us about who Jesus claims to be?

* How does God invite us to respond to our hunger and thirst (Isa. 55:2)? How does Jesus's invitation in John 6 compare?

_____

_____

* What kind of language is used to describe the food and drink in Isaiah 55? How would you characterize the emotion the passage conveys? What impact does the tone of Isaiah 55 have on the way you interpret Jesus's invitation in John 6?

_____

_____

_____

_____

* The Bible invites us to come and feast on the nourishing bread of life, but how do we actually do that? Read the verses below and write out practical ways to eat the bread Jesus provides.

Matthew 4:4:

_____

_____

Matthew 6:9–13:

_____

_____

1 Corinthians 11:23–26:

_____

_____

1 Peter 2:2:

_____

_____

💜 Memory Verse

"Jesus said to them, 'I am the bread of life; whoever comes to me shall not hunger, and whoever believes in me shall never thirst.'" *John 6:35*

APPLICATION: *How Do I Faithfully Respond?* The word of God doesn't just give us knowledge that stays in our heads; it gives us knowledge that changes our hearts. Today we'll focus on applying what we've learned this week to our own lives. Begin with prayer, asking God to encourage you, strengthen you, convict you of sin, instruct you, and reveal where he is leading you to grow.

In John 6, Jesus invites us to a meal—himself! Today we'll think about what that means for each of us as we taste and see that he is the food our souls desperately need.

1. The crowds wanted Jesus to meet their physical needs, but when he told them he could satisfy their greater spiritual need, they left. Do you tend to focus more on your physical needs or your spiritual needs? Think about your prayers. Are they typically more about life circumstances or spiritual concerns? (And we can take all our prayer requests to God—it just helps to think about what weighs on our heart the most!)

_____

_____

2. Jesus's followers asked a good question: "'What must we do, to be doing the works of God?' Jesus answered them, 'This is the work of God, that you believe in him whom he has sent'" (vv. 28–29). Have you believed in Jesus? Why or why not? In what ways are you tempted to work to get God's approval rather than believe by faith? What is the difference between the two? (See Eph. 2:8–10)

3. In what ways are you tempted to provide for yourself by working harder and doing more to prove yourself rather than trusting in Jesus for satisfaction and joy? What is one specific struggle on your heart today that you can take to Jesus in prayer, asking for him to provide?

4. Some Jews grumbled about Jesus's claim to be the bread of life from God, noting his questionable parentage. Others disputed what it meant theologically to eat his flesh. Even his own disciples said, "This is a hard saying" (v. 60), prompting Jesus to question if they wanted to leave. Write out how Peter responds. Following Jesus is not always easy. Sometimes it's really hard. If

someone asked you, "Why do you believe Jesus is the bread of life?" what would you say?

_____

_____

_____

_____

5. When we're hungry, our stomachs rumble, and we may become lightheaded or irritable. Spiritual hunger often shows up as discontentment, impatience, complaining, or unkindness. Where do you see signs of spiritual hunger in your own life? How can you treat your hunger as an invitation to feast?

_____

_____

_____

_____

6. In what false sources do you seek to satisfy your hunger and desires (for example, people, food, body image, adventures, alcohol, sex, or success)? How do you feel after you place your trust in those temporary satisfactions?

_____

_____

_____

_____

7. Just as we need food every day to sustain us and satisfy us, Jesus as the bread of life sustains and satisfies us day by day. What are a few specific ways you

can meet with Jesus throughout the day? What would it look like for you to eat the bread he is offering to you?

_____

_____

_____

_____

8. In what ways did this "I am" statement help you learn about Jesus?

What does it mean that Jesus is the bread of life?

_____

_____

How does Jesus ask you to respond?

_____

_____

What specific promise is associated with this "I am" statement?

_____

_____

Do you ever feel that no matter how much you fill up on the pleasures of this world, you're quickly hungry for more? We keep coming back to the same things to make us happy, or at least distract us from the pain, but no amount of scrolling, ice cream, or success can fully satisfy us (trust me, I've tried, especially the ice cream). Jesus calls us to stop scavenging and start feasting. Taste and see—he is so very good.

💜 **Memory Verse**

"Jesus said to them, 'I am the bread of life; whoever comes to me shall not hunger, and whoever believes in me shall never thirst.'" *John 6:35*

REFLECTION

I'll never forget the unmistakably salty taste of fresh Play-Doh. There's something about the bright colors that scream, "Taste me!" As a kid, I had my fair share of nibbles. Perhaps you too remember the briny taste and slimy texture. But the funny thing is, as a kid, I kept going back for more. *Maybe this time it will taste as good as it looks*, I thought. But I was always disappointed.

Expecting Play-Doh to taste delicious might sound silly, but when it comes to our spiritual food, we often look to things that can't meet our deepest needs.

Food has two major functions, to sustain and to satisfy. Food keeps us alive, but it is also a source of delight. But food isn't the only place we look for sustenance and delight. Too often we gulp down the hope of control, financial security, or well-thought-out plans to ensure life and safety for ourselves and those we love. Or maybe we feed on our own good works as if they can sustain us and help us earn life beyond the grave. We seek to satisfy our cravings by gorging ourselves on adventure, affection, comfort, or clout. But we are always left hungry for more. And our frail bodies and tragedy-marked world remind us at every turn that death is hunting us down. All our best efforts are never enough.

Jesus tells us that life and satisfaction are found only in him. He assures us, "Whoever comes to me shall not hunger, and whoever believes in me shall never thirst" (John 6:35).

Jesus is the bread of life. All who eat this bread overcome the seeming finality of death. Yes, our bodies decay and die, but that's not the end. Life is coming.

Jesus himself tasted death. Later in the Gospel of John, Jesus was beaten and bruised and nailed to a cross. The Son of God became a man and died in our place. Each of us deserves to die because each of us has sinned, and God in his perfect justice does not let the evils of sin go unpunished. But the one who was without sin—the one who calls himself the bread of life— experienced the fullness of death so that we might live. He paid the price of our sin on the cross, but his death was not final. Three days later, he rose from the dead. His resurrection is our hope: death has been defeated. And the resurrection is also John's final miraculous sign in his Gospel. It's the biggest proof that Jesus is exactly who he claimed to be—someone who has died and come back to life in three days is someone we want to learn more about!

When we nourish our souls with the bread of life, his resurrection life becomes our own. And Jesus tells us what it means to eat the bread of life: "Truly, truly, I say to you, whoever believes has eternal life" (John 6:47). If we believe that Jesus is the great I am, our Lord and Messiah who died to give us life, we will live forever. If we come to him and trust him as the only one who can save us from death, we will have eternal life.

The life Jesus gives is a future reality, but it is also something we can experience right now. Commentator Colin Kruse explains that "hunger and thirst are metaphors for the human need to know God, and knowing God is the present experience of eternal life."[1] Our longing for love, significance, happiness, comfort, and pleasure is ultimately only satisfied in God. Anything less is like chomping down on Play-Doh pizza—visually appealing but dreadfully deficient. Thankfully, we have access to the one who satisfies our hunger through Jesus Christ. John told us, "No one has ever seen God; the only God, who is at the Father's side, he has made him known" (John 1:18). To know Jesus is to know God. Our hunger for God is satisfied as the Spirit of Christ dwells in us. It's satisfied as we read the Bible, where God

---

1   Colin G. Kruse, *John: An Introduction and Commentary* (Downers Grove, IL: InterVarsity Press, 2017), 193.

reveals who he is. It's satisfied as we taste his goodness reflected in the good things he created.

Where are you turning to satisfy your hunger? Is it experiences or things that make you feel alive if only for a moment, or is it the bread of life that will never leave you hungry? Are you coming back to Play-Doh pies, or are you feasting on the bread of life?

1. In what areas of your life do you notice hunger or longing for more?

_____

_____

_____

_____

2. Do you tend to view eternal life as only a future promise? How might the truth that you can experience eternal life now by knowing God change the way you live?

_____

_____

_____

_____

💙 Memory Verse

"Jesus said to them, 'I am the bread of life; whoever comes to me shall not hunger, and whoever believes in me shall never thirst.'" *John 6:35*

DISCUSSION QUESTIONS

Icebreaker: What's your favorite meal when you are really hungry?

Warm-up: How does being physically hungry impact the way you feel and act?

1. Read John 6:25–71. Jesus claims, "I am the bread of life." From your study this week, what does that mean? Why do you think he described himself in that way at this moment in the story?

2. In what ways is Jesus as the bread of life better than the manna in the wilderness?

3. Think through the Jews, the disciples, and the people listening to Jesus's teaching. How did the different people respond? How do you see differing responses to Jesus in our world today? Does Peter's response to Jesus resonate with you? Why or why not?

_____

_____

_____

4. What does Jesus say is the work of God (v. 29)? Why is this so difficult for us? How do we try to find favor with God by our own works? Does this mean our good works don't matter? (See Eph. 2:8–10)

_____

_____

_____

_____

5. The crowds came to Jesus to meet their physical needs, but when he told them he could satisfy their greater spiritual need, they left. Do you tend to focus more on your physical needs or your spiritual needs?

_____

_____

_____

_____

6. In what sources do you seek to satisfy your hunger and desires (for example, people, food, body image, adventures, alcohol, sex, or success)? How do you feel after you place your trust in those temporary satisfactions?

_____

_____

_____

_____

7. How did this text help you see, believe, and live?

What did you see or learn about Jesus?

_____

_____

What do you need to believe as a result?

_____

_____

How should you live in response?

_____

_____

8. What was one thing from this study that encouraged, convicted, or instructed you this week?

_____

_____

_____

_____

2

I Am the Light of the World

L ast week Jesus introduced himself to us as the bread of life. He told us about the life-giving nourishment and satisfaction available in himself. This week we'll hear how he offers a solution not only to hunger but also to darkness.

Darkness is familiar. Whether we experience the literal darkness after dusk or the weight of a world darkened by evil, we have all become, as Robert Frost put it, "acquainted with the night."[1] Darkness comes in many forms. You might be acquainted with the darkness of depression or grief. Maybe you know the darkness of persistent sin—yours or that of someone close to you. Most of us have experienced the darkness of confusion and chaos. We've all been impacted by the darkness and brokenness of this world.

But this week we will see that the light of the world has come. God is the light that shatters the darkness. John began his Gospel by telling us, "The light shines in the darkness, and the darkness has not overcome it" (John 1:5). As the light of the world, Jesus illuminates the darkness. He gives hope, healing,

---

1 Robert Frost, "Acquainted with the Night," Poetry Foundation, accessed August 18, 2022, https://www .poetryfoundation.org/.

comfort, cleansing, and clarity. And one glorious day, when we see him face-to-face, there will be no darkness at all.

⬆ Prayer for the Week

Lord, illuminate my heart and mind to understand your word. Help me see the truth about who Jesus is, that I may know him and know you who sent him. Guide me to walk in the light. In Jesus's name I pray, Amen.

💜 Memory Verse

"Again Jesus spoke to them, saying, 'I am the light of the world. Whoever follows me will not walk in darkness, but will have the light of life.'" *John 8:12*

OBSERVATION
What Does the Text Say?

John 8:12–47

Again Jesus spoke to them, saying, "I am the light of the world. Whoever follows me will not walk in darkness, but will have the light of life." So the Pharisees said to him, "You are bearing witness about yourself; your testimony is not true." Jesus answered, "Even if I do bear witness about myself, my testimony is true, for I know where I came from and where I am going, but you do not know where I come from or where I am going. You judge according to the flesh; I judge no one. Yet even if I do judge, my judgment is true, for it is not I alone who judge, but I and the Father who sent me. In your Law it is written that the testimony of two people is true. I am the one who bears witness about myself, and the Father who sent me bears witness about me." They said to him therefore, "Where is your Father?" Jesus answered, "You know neither me nor my Father. If you knew me, you would know my Father also." These words he spoke in the treasury, as he taught in the temple; but no one arrested him, because his hour had not yet come.

So he said to them again, "I am going away, and you will seek me, and you will die in your sin. Where I am going, you cannot come." So the Jews said, "Will he kill himself, since he says, 'Where I am going, you cannot come'?" He said to them, "You are from below; I am from above. You are of this world; I am not of this world. I told you that you would die in your sins, for unless you believe that I am he you will die in your sins." So they said to him, "Who are you?" Jesus said to them, "Just what I have been telling you from the beginning. I have much to say about you and much to judge, but he who sent me is true, and I declare to the world what I have heard from him." They did not understand that he had been speaking to them about the Father. So Jesus said to them, "When you have lifted up the Son of Man, then you will know that I am he, and that I do nothing on my own authority, but speak just as the Father taught me. And he who sent me is with me. He has not left me alone, for I always do the things that are pleasing to him." As he was saying these things, many believed in him.

So Jesus said to the Jews who had believed him, "If you abide in my word, you are truly my disciples, and you will know the truth, and the truth will set you free." They answered him, "We are offspring of Abraham and have never been enslaved to anyone. How is it that you say, 'You will become free'?"

Jesus answered them, "Truly, truly, I say to you, everyone who practices sin is a slave to sin. The slave does not remain in the house forever; the son remains forever. So if the Son sets you free, you will be free indeed. I know that you are offspring of Abraham; yet you seek to kill me because my word finds no place in you. I speak of what I have seen with my Father, and you do what you have heard from your father."

They answered him, "Abraham is our father." Jesus said to them, "If you were Abraham's children, you would be doing the works Abraham did, but now you seek to kill me, a man who has told you the truth that I heard from God. This is not what Abraham did. You are doing the works your father did." They said to him, "We were not born of sexual immorality. We have one Father—even God." Jesus said to them, "If God were your Father, you would love me, for I came from God and I am here. I came not of my own accord, but he sent me. Why do you not understand what I say? It is because you cannot bear to hear my word. You are of your father the devil, and your will is to do your father's desires. He was a murderer from the beginning, and does not stand in the truth, because there is no truth in him. When he lies, he speaks out of his own character, for he is a liar and the father of lies. But because I tell the truth, you do not believe me. Which one of you convicts me of sin? If I tell the truth, why do you not believe me? Whoever is of God hears the words of God. The reason why you do not hear them is that you are not of God."

———

This week we join Jesus in Jerusalem for the Feast of Tabernacles, where Jews gathered to remember how God delivered them out of slavery in Egypt. The festival included lighting four huge lamps whose flames could be seen for miles, while attendees danced and celebrated with torches in hand.[2] On the last night of the festival, surrounded by great lights, Jesus declared, "I am the light of the world."

Begin your time with prayer and then read John 8:12–47.

1. Read Jesus's "I am" statement in verse 12.

   What did Jesus claim to be?

   _____

   _____

   What did Jesus say is the result of following him?

   _____

   _____

---

2 D. A. Carson, *The Gospel according to John* (Grand Rapids, MI: Eerdmans, 1991), 337.

How did Jesus describe the light he offers?

_____

_____

2. When Jesus fed five thousand people, his miraculous sign was proof for his claim to be the bread of life. According to the verses below, what did Jesus give as evidence for his second "I am" statement?

vv. 17–18

_____

_____

v. 28

_____

_____

v. 29

_____

_____

3. Now read John 9:1–7. How does Jesus's healing of the man born blind offer proof for his claim in the previous chapter to be the light of the world?

_____

_____

4. The text distinguishes between two opposing paths, and repeated words help us see those paths. Highlight or underline each of the following groups of words in a different color in the printed text:

Forms of the words *true, know, hear,* and *believe*

Forms of the words *lie, sin,* and *die*

5. Opposition to Jesus was growing, and Jesus wasn't afraid to acknowledge it. In fact, he sought to show his opponents that they chose the wrong side. Use the chart below to note the times Jesus contrasted himself with the Pharisees and other unbelieving Jews.

Jesus	The Jews
(v. 14) I know where I came from and where I am going	(v. 14) You do not know where I come from or where I am going
(v. 15) You judge according to the flesh	(v. 15)
(v. 18) The Father who sent me bears witness about me	(v. 19)

Jesus	The Jews
(v. 21) I am going away	(v. 21)
(v. 23) I am from above	(v. 23)
(v. 23) I am not of this world	(v. 23)

6. The path of life we choose has consequences, whether positive or negative. Jesus said that everyone walks one of two paths: the path of light or the path of darkness. What did Jesus say are the results of the actions or states below?

The path of light:

following Jesus (v. 12):

knowing Jesus (v. 19):

being true disciples of Jesus (v. 31):

abiding in Jesus's word (vv. 31–32):

knowing the truth (v. 32):

being a son (v. 35):

being "of God" (v. 47):

The path of darkness:

not believing in Jesus (v. 24):

practicing sin (v. 34):

being a slave to sin (v. 35):

_____

_____

7. The Jews claimed that God was their Father, but Jesus said the devil was their father. According to Jesus, what characterizes someone who is a child of God and someone who is a child of the devil? (See vv. 39–47)

_____

_____

_____

_____

8. Did anything about Jesus or his interactions with others surprise you in this passage? What are some questions you have about the story?

_____

_____

_____

_____

At first glance, Jesus's claim to be the light of the world may seem disconnected from the rest of the dialogue, but when we look closer, we see that Jesus used the rest of the chapter to paint two pictures: what it looks like to walk in darkness and what it looks like to have the light of life. Jesus didn't sugarcoat his message, and you may find his words shocking or even offensive. They are confrontational and convicting, but they also offer great hope—hope of freedom from sin and life found in the light of the world. As we continue studying, we'll take a deeper look at why this is good news.

🤍 **Memory Verse**

"Again Jesus spoke to them, saying, 'I am the light of the world. Whoever follows me will not walk in darkness, but will have the light of life.'" *John 8:12*

INTERPRETATION
What Does the Text Mean?

We've spent time noticing important details in the text, so now it's time to evaluate what the text means in light of what we've observed. Read the passage again today before moving on to the questions below. Begin your time with prayer, asking God to give you wisdom as you study.

Read John 8:12–47.

1. What are possible challenges or dangers of walking at night without a light? How does that help you understand verse 12?

---

2. Look back at the words you highlighted yesterday. What do these repeated words reveal about what it means to walk in the darkness and to have the light of life? What are the final destinations of these two paths?

The Pharisees were Jewish religious leaders who studied and taught God's word. Many prided themselves on strict adherence to the law and superior knowledge of God. Maybe those Pharisees and religious leaders remind you of someone you know, or maybe, if you're honest, you see yourself in them. They thought they were enlightened, but Jesus frequently rebuked them for their prideful self-reliance and poor treatment of others. He described them not as people of light and truth like they thought, but as people of darkness and lies.

Citing the Old Testament requirement for at least two witnesses in any court case (Num. 35:30), the Pharisees accused Jesus of falsehood and sought to discredit his claim to be the light of the world on the grounds that he needed another witness.

3. Why would Jesus be exempt from needing a second human witness? What does Jesus's response reveal about who he is? (vv. 14–18)

4. Look back at the chart you completed yesterday contrasting Jesus with the Pharisees and unbelieving Jews. How was Jesus challenging what the Jews believed about themselves? If Jesus were talking to us today, what beliefs about ourselves do you think he would challenge?

5. The man born blind in John 9 suffered from physical blindness. In what ways does Jesus expose the spiritual blindness of the Pharisees in this passage?

_____

_____

_____

_____

6. In verse 31, Jesus said those who are truly his disciples aren't those who seem religious on the outside but are those who abide in his word. What do the following verses say about what it means to abide in Jesus's word?

John 14:15:

_____

_____

John 14:21:

_____

_____

John 14:23–24:

_____

_____

John 15:10:

_____

_____

7. John 8:32 says, "You will know the truth, and the truth will set you free." From what did Jesus promise freedom? Read the verses before and after verse 32 to help you answer. How is this kind of freedom different from the world's idea of freedom?

---

8. What warning and invitation should we take from this passage?

Has anyone ever encouraged you to follow your own path? Your life, your story, your way, right? Not according to Jesus. Instead, Jesus presented two paths: the way of darkness and the way of light. The Pharisees thought they were the enlightened ones, but they fooled themselves and others. They were walking in darkness and missed the only true light—they missed Jesus. The light of the world calls us to believe in him, follow him, and be free from slavery to sin. Which path are you taking?

🩶 Memory Verse

"Again Jesus spoke to them, saying, 'I am the light of the world. Whoever follows me will not walk in darkness, but will have the light of life.'" *John 8:12*

INTERPRETATION
What Does the Whole Bible Say?

John 8 isn't the first time light shows up in Scripture. In fact, it's a significant theme that runs through the whole Bible! Today we are going to trace the theme of light as it unfolds throughout the Bible to give us a fuller understanding of Jesus's claim to be the light of the world. Begin your time by praying for God to illuminate your heart and mind as you read his word, and then read John 8:12–47 again before answering the questions below.

1. Read Genesis 1:1–5.

What was the earth like before the first day of creation?

_____

_____

How was the light created, and what do we learn about it?

_____

_____

_____

_____

God is the source of all light. He created light and is the one who sends it into the world. The first light he sent brought life and flourishing where there was emptiness and chaos. God filled the world with not only physical light but spiritual light as well—the light of knowing God, walking in his ways, and enjoying his presence. But it wasn't long before darkness entered. The first humans, Adam and Eve, disobeyed God's commands. Their sin brought spiritual darkness into their hearts and all of creation. But God had a plan to overcome the darkness with light.

2. Read Exodus 13:17–22. God had just delivered the Israelites out of slavery in Egypt. What was the purpose of the pillar of fire?

_____

_____

_____

_____

3. Read Psalm 119:105. What metaphor is used to describe God's word? In what ways does God's word lead and guide us?

_____

_____

_____

_____

4. Isaiah 9:2–7 was a prophecy spoken to the Israelites, who were rejecting God, to tell them of the judgment they would endure. God was going to send this judgment to bring his people to repentance and back to him. Read the passage and then answer the following questions.

What are the effects of the light promised in verse 2?

_____

_____

What event marks the coming of the light? See verses 6–7.

_____

_____

What similarities do you see between Isaiah 9:2 and John 8:12? Why do you think these similarities are significant?

_____

_____

Just as God's presence lit the way for his people in the wilderness, his word offers light to guide us. The Old Testament promised and anticipated the light that would shine in the darkness. Now let's consider how John announces the arrival of the long-expected light in the New Testament.

5. Read John 1:1–13.

According to verse 4, what is the light?

_____

_____

Why did John bear witness about the light?

_____

_____

What is the result of believing in the light?

_____

_____

What similarities do you see between this passage and the Old Testament passages we read?

_____

_____

As the light of the world, Jesus is God's presence with us to guide us, heal us, and give us life and flourishing. He is the Word of God become flesh—the very Word that was with God in the beginning, bringing light into the darkness and guiding people into truth. He has come, and he leads us in the way of light. We still see all kinds of darkness everywhere in our world, but one day that will change.

6. Revelation 21 is a prophecy about the future new creation and uses imagery to describe what the world will be like when Jesus comes back and makes everything new. Read Revelation 21:22–25.

Who is the lamb? See John 1:29 for help.

_____

_____

What similarities and differences do you see between the light in this passage and the light in Genesis 1:1–5?

_____

_____

What similarities and differences do you see between this passage and John 8:12?

_____

_____

It can be easy to become overwhelmed when we see the darkness all around us—on the news, in our homes, even in our own bodies—but the darkness cannot overcome the light! Throughout the Old Testament, God promised light that would illuminate even the darkest places. Year after year, God's people waited. Jesus's announcement that he is the light of the world is not merely a helpful image but the fulfillment of a promise God made from the beginning. The light has come, and the light is coming. We can walk in the light now and for all eternity when we know the light of the world. He offers life, guidance, hope, and healing (Mal. 4:2).

💜 Memory Verse

"Again Jesus spoke to them, saying, 'I am the light of the world. Whoever follows me will not walk in darkness, but will have the light of life.'" *John 8:12*

APPLICATION: *How Do I Faithfully Respond?* We've seen that the light Jesus shines into our lives does several things. It illuminates our path, exposes what is hidden in darkness, and brings flourishing, healing, and life. Jesus's identity as the light of the world has major implications for the way we live. Today we will examine our hearts and lives in light of those truths. Pray for God to encourage you, reveal sin in your life, transform your heart, and give you wisdom about how to respond to his word. Before you answer today's questions, reread John 8:12–47.

1. Jesus explained that obedience to God's word is evidence that someone is walking in the light, while disobedience is like walking in darkness. Take a moment to honestly evaluate your life—your thoughts, your actions, and how you spend your time and money. Is your life marked by a pattern of obedience to God's word or by a pattern of disobedience?

_____

_____

_____

_____

2. The Pharisees thought they were walking in the light because they knew a lot about the Bible, did religious things, and came from a specific family. However, Jesus challenged their assumptions about themselves and told them they had to believe in him. It can be easy to think we are in a good place because we try to treat others with kindness, know a lot about the Bible, or grew up in church. What do you tend to depend upon to put you in good standing with God? How do you think Jesus would challenge you?

_____

_____

_____

_____

3. Jesus described sin as something that enslaves us. When we are enslaved to something, it's our master, and we must do what it tells us. Read Romans 6:20–23. Sometimes doing the sinful things we want to do feels like freedom, but they lead to death. Do you recognize any persistent sin in your life that is controlling you instead of giving freedom? What is it?

_____

_____

_____

_____

4. In the Bible, God gives us everything we need to know to walk the path of light (2 Pet. 1:3). What practical steps can you take this week to spend time in Scripture as you seek to abide in Jesus's word?

5. Our study of darkness and light throughout the rest of Scripture revealed that spiritual darkness takes many forms, such as evil, pain, chaos, and suffering. How do you see this kind of darkness impacting you? How does the light of Jesus give you hope in those places even as the darkness remains?

6. God's word is described as a guiding lamp for our paths. Where specifically do you need God's guidance right now? Where do you tend to turn first for answers or help when you face challenges in your life (for example, do you turn to the internet, a friend, or your own strength)? What would it look like practically to seek help and guidance from the light of the world first?

7. In what ways did this "I am" statement help you learn about Jesus?

What does it mean that Jesus is the light of the world?

_____

_____

How does Jesus ask you to respond?

_____

_____

What specific promise is associated with this "I am" statement?

_____

_____

As you considered what path you're headed down, was it difficult to take an honest look at your life? It can be hard to see our own sins or needs or the assumptions we have about ourselves, but we can pray and ask God to reveal those things to us.

After Jesus declared, "I am the light of the world," he healed a man who was blind from birth. All the man had seen was darkness until Jesus opened his eyes to see the light. But Jesus did more than give the blind man physical sight. He went to the man a second time and revealed himself as the promised Savior. The light of the world opened the eyes of the blind man to see and believe in Jesus.

When we come to the light of the world, our vision is transformed. Apart from Jesus, because of our sin, we walk unknowingly like blind men, but when he opens our eyes, he illuminates everything. We were blind to his goodness, blind to our need for him, and blind to the hope he offers. But when we believe in the light of the world, we can say with the man born blind, "Though I was blind, now I see" (9:25).

Memory Verse

"Again Jesus spoke to them, saying, 'I am the light of the world. Whoever follows me will not walk in darkness, but will have the light of life.'" *John 8:12*

REFLECTION

I recently attended a women's retreat in the mountains with my local church. I shared a lower-level room in a cabin with three other women. The deceptively decorative curtains on the wall caused me to overlook the fact that there was not a single window downstairs. When we turned the lights off the first night, I realized just how dark it was. I expected my eyes to adjust and begin to make out shapes after a few minutes, but there was no light to adjust to. It was a bit unsettling.

Later that night I awoke needing to use the bathroom.

As I made my way out of the bedroom, I knew I just had to walk a few feet forward to find the bathroom. I shuffled blindly with my hands stretched out in front of me feeling for the door frame. I found it relatively quickly, but when I reached for the light switch, it was as if it had disappeared. I slid my hand up and down and across the wall with no luck, so I started feeling for something else—the toilet, the sink, the tub—anything to help reorient myself in total darkness. I searched for what felt like 10 minutes, but all I found was a blank wall. I was completely turned around. I wondered, *Where am I? Am I going to be stuck here all night? How will I find my way back?* I was lost without any light to guide me.

Eventually I used my phone's flashlight and saw that I didn't know the way to the bathroom as well as I thought. The door I had entered across the hall didn't lead to the bathroom, but was the entrance to a large corridor. I was so sure I knew the way, but it turns out I was groping for objects in an empty room.

The Pharisees believed they knew the way to abundant and eternal life. Most of them trusted in their good works, DNA, or scholarly knowledge to put them in right relationship with God. But Jesus told them their lives indicated otherwise. They were walking in darkness, confident they possessed the way to life but blindly strolling down the path to death.

When we sin against God—choosing our way over his way—we are walking in darkness. We might think we are on the right path, but our sins of pride, greed, and selfishness are leading us astray. Without Jesus, our hearts are darkened, and we can't find the path of true joy.

Are you weary from groping in the darkness only to find the fulfillment you're seeking isn't there at all? Are you discouraged because every time you think you've found the path to happiness and purpose you end up more lost than when you started? The world promises new ways to abundant life around every corner, but they are counterfeit luminaries. We don't need to do more, be more, have more—we need the true light that has come into the world.

1. If you're honest, how would you complete this sentence? "If I had _____, then I would experience abundant life."

_____

_____

_____

_____

2. Are there any areas of your life where you find it hard to believe that God's way is the better way? How so?

_____

_____

💜 **Memory Verse**

"Again Jesus spoke to them, saying, 'I am the light of the world. Whoever follows me will not walk in darkness, but will have the light of life.'" *John 8:12*

DISCUSSION QUESTIONS

Icebreaker: What's the most creative thing you've used for light when your electricity has gone out?

Warm-up: Can you share a time when you got hurt because you couldn't see where you were going?

1. Read John 8:12–47. How would you describe the two paths Jesus presented? Make two lists of words that describe the path of darkness and the path of light.

2. What warning and invitation should we take from this week's passage? What are some specific areas in our lives where the warning applies? What would it look like practically to respond to Jesus's invitation?

_____

_____

_____

_____

3. What did you learn this week about who Jesus claims to be? What evidence do you see to support those claims? Do you find the evidence convincing?

_____

_____

_____

_____

4. Based on the passages you read on Day 3, why is Jesus's claim to be the light of the world in John 8 so significant? How do these passages give you hope for the specific darkness you see around you?

_____

_____

_____

_____

5. How would you complete the following sentence? "If I were truly free, my life would look like _____." Does your idea of freedom align with the one Jesus described, or is it different? How so?

_____

_____

_____

_____

6. Share how God's word has been a lamp to guide your path. Where do you tend to turn first for answers or help when you face challenges in your life (for example, do you turn to the internet, a friend, or your own strength)? What would it look like to seek help and guidance from the light of the world first?

_____

_____

_____

_____

7. How did this text help you see, believe, and live?

What did you see or learn about Jesus?

_____

_____

What do you need to believe as a result?

_____

_____

How should you live in response?

_____

_____

8. What was one thing that encouraged, convicted, or instructed you this week?

_____

_____

_____

_____

3

I Am the Door

As a child I watched a game show that presented contestants with three doors—door number one, door number two, and door number three. Behind only one of the doors was a prize, and it was the contestant's job to pick the winning door. The contestant would almost always hesitate, start to pick one, change her mind, select another, and then nervously sit back to see if she had selected the one door with the prize behind it. If she had chosen correctly, when the door was opened, there was something spectacular waiting for her. But if she chose the wrong door, she went home empty-handed.

Aren't you glad that salvation isn't a guessing game? There are not multiple doors. There is one door—and his name is Jesus.

This week as we study Jesus's third "I am" statement—"I am the door"—we will see that in Jesus, there are blessings and joys greater than anything this world can offer. If you are new to thinking about Jesus, this might seem too good to be true. But as we look at John 10, we will see that Jesus is always more and better than we ever imagine.

⬆ Prayer

Father, I come to you knowing that you not only have the words of life; your Son is the Word of life. As I study this week, help me understand what it means that Jesus is the door. Use this time I'll spend in your word to strengthen my faith and help me love Jesus more. Thank you for meeting me by your Spirit in your living word. In Jesus's name, Amen.

💜 Memory Verse

"[Jesus said,] 'I am the door. If anyone enters by me, he will be saved and will go in and out and find pasture.'" *John 10:9*

OBSERVATION
What Does the Text Say?

John 10:1-10

"Truly, truly, I say to you, he who does not enter the sheepfold by the door but climbs in by another way, that man is a thief and a robber. But he who enters by the door is the shepherd of the sheep. To him the gatekeeper opens. The sheep hear his voice, and he calls his own sheep by name and leads them out. When he has brought out all his own, he goes before them, and the sheep follow him, for they know his voice. A stranger they will not follow, but they will flee from him, for they do not know the voice of strangers." This figure of speech Jesus used with them, but they did not understand what he was saying to them.

So Jesus again said to them, "Truly, truly, I say to you, I am the door of the sheep. All who came before me are thieves and robbers, but the sheep did not listen to them. I am the door. If anyone enters by me, he will be saved and will go in and out and find pasture. The thief comes only to steal and kill and destroy. I came that they may have life and have it abundantly."

This week we'll be studying the third "I am" statement: "I am the door." Some translations use the word *gate* instead of *door*, but the words serve the same purpose; Jesus was referring to what allowed entrance into a sheep pen.

As we observe the passage, try to imagine or visualize the scenes Jesus paints with his words. Picture the sheep going in and out of a pen, shepherds leading them, and thieves trying to steal them. Imagine what the sheepfolds (or sheep pens) looked like. I'll include some historical details that will help us imagine it faithfully. The whole passage will become richer if we spend time visualizing the images Jesus created with his words.

1. To whom was Jesus speaking in this passage? You might need to go back and skim John 9 to answer this. And it might help to know that in "John's gospel the term 'Jews,' often represents the religious hierarchy in Jerusalem who tended to oppose Jesus and his message."[1]

2. List the characters (people and animals) Jesus described in this passage.

1 Robert W. Yarbrough, *John: With a New Preface and Bibliography* (Eugene, OR: Wipf & Stock, 2011), 106–7.

3. What are the two ways into the sheep pen, and who utilizes each way?

4. There are two separate scenes in this passage. The first is found in verses 1–5; the second is found in verses 7–10. Briefly summarize each scene in your own words.

Scene 1 (vv. 1–5)	Scene 2 (vv. 7–10)

There were most likely two types of sheep pens in ancient Israel. Verses 1–5 probably refer to the type of sheep pen found in villages and towns.[2] These pens were often made from a room or courtyard on the exterior of a home.[3] This type of sheep pen usually had a door or gate for the sheep to go through as they came in at night and went out in the morning. Because it was in a village, and almost every family would have owned at least a few sheep, several families would share a sheep pen. The gatekeeper was the one responsible for making sure he opened the gate only to the legitimate shepherd and not to a

---

2   Kenneth E. Bailey, *The Good Shepherd: A Thousand-Year Journey from Psalm 23 to the New Testament* (Downers Grove, IL: IVP Academic, 2014), 211.

3   James Montgomery Boice, *The Gospel of John: An Expositional Commentary* (Grand Rapids, MI: Baker, 2005), 737.

thief or robber. It was the shepherd's job to call out the sheep entrusted to his care, and the sheep were to follow their shepherd.

The other type of sheep pen was found in the countryside and was usually not much more than a bunch of stones gathered and piled in a circle. Verses 7–10 probably envision this type of sheep pen. Occasionally, the "pen" would be made using the side of a cliff. But it was common for the opening *not* to have an actual gate or door. Instead, the shepherd watching over the sheep—usually the son of the man who owned the sheep—would lie down across the opening.[4] His body was, in fact, the door to the pen, used to keep the sheep in and the thieves out.

5. Verses 3–5 describe the different relationships between the sheep and the voices they might hear. What two ways do the sheep interact with the shepherd's voice?

What do the sheep do when they hear a stranger's voice?

Why?

What is the key difference that determines who the sheep will follow?

---

4 Colin G. Kruse, *John: An Introduction and Commentary* (Downers Grove, IL: InterVarsity Press, 2017), 267.

6. What two things happen for those who enter by the door (v. 9)? Compare this with what the thief does (v. 10).

_____

_____

_____

_____

7. Write down any other observations or questions you have about the passage.

_____

_____

_____

_____

I'm assuming that not many of us are shepherds. If you are, I would love to spend a day following you around and learning more about sheep and the people they follow! But, until then, and for the rest of us, spend some time today reflecting on the scenes Jesus painted. As you work on your memory verse, picture the sheep going in and going out. Ask the Lord to give you insight and understanding as you study his word.

💜 Memory Verse

"[Jesus said,] 'I am the door. If anyone enters by me, he will be saved and will go in and out and find pasture.'" *John 10:9*

INTERPRETATION

What Does the Text Mean?

Metaphors are meant to be interpreted. Jesus was not talking about sheepfolds and doors in order to instruct shepherds. He was using the story to communicate a deeper, spiritual truth. It's the job of the listener or reader to ask the Holy Spirit to help us discern those greater truths. That's what we will do today, whether you've known Jesus for a long time or are learning about him for the first time. Ask the Lord to open your eyes so that you can see the beauty of what he wants us to understand.

1. Yesterday you listed all the characters you found in this passage (Q2). Today explain who or what you think they each represent and why.

2. Describe what a door is and does. In what ways does this help you understand why Jesus called himself the door?

3. Describe what you think Jesus meant (and what he didn't mean) when he said, "I came that they may have life and have it abundantly" (v. 10). Is he talking about eternal life, life here and now, both, or neither? Explain why.

4. Who do you think Jesus was referring to when he said, "All who came before me are thieves and robbers" (v. 8)? Why do you think this?

5. Jesus said that the sheep know their shepherd's voice and follow it. Conversely, they don't know the voice of a stranger, so they flee from it. What do you think Jesus meant for the people listening, and what do you think it means for us today?

6. Why do you think Jesus's audience did not understand what he was saying (v. 6)?

_____

_____

_____

_____

7. What do you think might be some of Jesus's main points in this passage? What makes you think this?

_____

_____

_____

_____

Shepherds in the ancient Near East didn't drive their sheep from behind; they led them from in front by singing or calling to them as they walked.[5] I once saw a video where a man was standing by a gate to a yard that contained eight dogs. He opened the gate and proceeded to call each dog by name. As he called a name, the dog with that name ran out of the gate and to the man. It was a beautiful picture of one of the points Jesus is making in this passage—he knows you and calls you by name! Never cease to be amazed that the Creator of the world calls you by name. Run to him. Follow where he leads.

💜 Memory Verse

"[Jesus said,] 'I am the door. If anyone enters by me, he will be saved and will go in and out and find pasture.'" _John 10:9_

---

5 Andreas J. Köstenberger, _John_, Baker Exegetical Commentary (Grand Rapids, MI: Baker, 2004), 301.

INTERPRETATION
What Does the Whole Bible Say?

Today we will look at both some Old Testament and New Testament passages to see if we can gain more understanding on John 10:1-10.

1. Read Psalm 100:3-4. What similarities do you see between this passage and John 10:1-10? (Remember that *gate* and *door* mean basically the same thing.)

2. Read Ezekiel 34:1-10. We'll study this passage again next week, but for now, how does this help us better understand John 10:8? Using the words and images Ezekiel used, fill in the chart below.

What a Good Shepherd Does	What a Wicked Shepherd Does

3. Read Psalm 118:19–22. The gates referred to in this psalm are the gates that led into the temple. Anybody who wanted to worship God would have to go through these gates. How does this passage help us better understand Jesus as the gate?

_____

_____

_____

_____

Now let's turn to the New Testament.

4. Read Hebrews 10:19–20. How do these verses increase our understanding of John 10:9?

_____

_____

_____

_____

5. Read Matthew 7:13–14 and Acts 4:12. What do these verses add to our understanding of Jesus as the door or gate? What is Jesus leading us into?

_____

_____

_____

_____

6. Matthew 25:1–13 tells the story of an invitation to a wedding feast. It is a parable about entrance into the kingdom of heaven. In verse 10, what do you learn about the door, and how might this compel you to share the gospel with someone?

_____

_____

_____

_____

7. When you go through customs in the airport, you have to pass through a gate, proving your citizenship before you are allowed to enter the country. Read Ephesians 2:18–19. What type of citizenship does Jesus offer us? What does that mean for us? How does that relate to John 10:1–10?

_____

_____

_____

_____

There is a door. There is a gate. There is salvation. His name is Jesus and the door is still open! If you have not yet entered his gates with thanksgiving and his courts with praise, if you have not yet become part of the household of God, today is a great day to do that. The gate may be narrow, but it leads to the wide-open space of abundant life—both now and forever.

💜 Memory Verse

"[Jesus said,] 'I am the door. If anyone enters by me, he will be saved and will go in and out and find pasture.'" _John 10:9_

APPLICATION: *How Do I Faithfully Respond?* As we seek to apply this passage to our lives, the first thing we need to do is praise God that there is a door! Jesus isn't sharing these "I am" statements with us for his benefit; he's telling us the good news so we might respond by faith to his invitation and his promises.

1. The most important question you can answer is, "Have I entered into relationship with God through the one and only door he has provided—his Son?" If you can answer yes, write a prayer of praise thanking him for giving us a way to be saved. If not, write a prayer asking God to show you your need and give you the gift of faith. He will hear and be faithful to you!

_____

_____

_____

_____

The second thing we need to recognize is that we are the sheep in Jesus's metaphor. It will be helpful to think about what the sheep were doing, what they needed, what dangers threatened them, and how the shepherd cared for them.

2. What is true of the sheep that is also true of you and me?

_____

_____

_____

_____

The sheep in our passage were vulnerable to getting lost, being led astray, and getting injured. Are you in danger of any of these spiritually? What are examples of modern-day thieves that can lead us spiritually astray?

We see in Jesus's story in John 10 that the shepherd protected and provided for his sheep. How has God done these things for you?

3. How do you think the sheep learned the sound of their shepherd's voice?

What are the implications for you?

_____

_____

Verse 3 says that the sheep *hear* the voice of their shepherd, and verse 4 says that they *know* the voice of their shepherd. What is the difference between hearing and knowing?

What was the result of knowing his voice?

_____

_____

I once heard a pastor say, "If you want to hear God speak, read the Bible out loud." He wasn't wrong! The Bible is the word of God and is the way and the place he has chosen to speak to us. The temptation for all of us is to think that the Lord speaks to us through our conscience, our gut, or our heart. But we need to remember that if what we "feel" contradicts the written word of God, then we are wrong—because the word of God is always true. Which means, in order to know God's voice, we have to know his word because his word is where he has chosen to speak.

4. Have you ever watched children run the opposite direction after they hear their teacher calling them to come in from the playground? They may have heard their teacher's voice, but they didn't obey. Is there a part of the Bible (Jesus's word to us) that you've heard but you don't want to obey? Confess that to Jesus today, trusting in the promise of James 5:16. Ask Jesus to give you the strength to follow him, even when the road is narrow and difficult.

5. Because we're like sheep, we will all follow something or someone. Some voices are wise and point us back to Jesus. Other voices can lead us astray. What voices seek your attention or allegiance? Where do they lead? Are you listening to any voices that you need to flee from?

6. How do Jesus's words—"He calls his own sheep by name" (v. 3)—comfort or encourage you?

7. At this point, we've studied three "I am" statements. Let's look at them again together to review what we've learned so far.

- "I am the living bread that came down from heaven. If anyone eats of this bread, he will live forever." (John 6:51)

- "Again Jesus spoke to them, saying, 'I am the light of the world. Whoever follows me will not walk in darkness, but will have the light of life.'" (John 8:12)

- "I am the door. If anyone enters by me, he will be saved and will go in and out and find pasture." (John 10:9)

Fill out the following chart, noting that each time Jesus tells us about himself, he invites us to respond, and he gives a promise to anyone who responds.

Verse	"I Am" Statement	Personal Response	Promise Given
John 6:51	I am living bread	Eat the bread	Lives forever

How do these verses invite you to specifically respond to Jesus today? What promises encourage you today?

_____

_____

8. In what ways did this "I am" statement help you learn about Jesus?

What does it mean that Jesus is the door or gate?

_____

_____

How does Jesus ask you to respond?

_____

_____

What specific promise is associated with this "I am" statement?

_____

_____

💙 Memory Verse

"[Jesus said,] 'I am the door. If anyone enters by me, he will be saved and will go in and out and find pasture.'" *John 10:9*

CCCCC

Day 5

REFLECTION

Have you ever seen a person who is blind learn to downhill ski? I have, and it's one of the bravest and most amazing things I've ever seen! Several years ago while I was on vacation, I noticed a ski school for children who have vision impairments. For the first day or two, the group just spent time with their instructor at the base of the mountain. She told them what skiing was like, what to expect, and how they would learn.

By day three, the students were ready to take the chairlift and head up the mountain. At first, each skier took a turn with the instructor. The child stood with her skis forming a wedge. The instructor put her skis on the outside of the child's skis and put her arms around the child's waist. At this point, they were ready to slowly go down the slope. As her skis guided the student's skis, the instructor talked to the skier the whole time—*careful, right, left, stop; right, left, stop*. The instructor helped the child avoid other skiers and tune out the other noises on the slope.

But by day four, the situation had changed. The instructor no longer skied with the child. Instead, she stood at the top of the slope and slowly spoke her instructions as the child navigated the slope alone, calling out the whole time, *slowly, right, left, right, left, stop; right, left, stop*. Each child made it down the slope!

By the end of the week, the skiers had picked up speed. The instructor still stood at the top of the slope, giving clear instruction, but the pace was much faster—*right, left, right, left, right, left, right, left*. And the skier was able to turn on a dime as she listened carefully to her instructor's voice and tuned out all the other voices on the slope. The joy for each skier was obvious. Each one seemed to feel the sun on her face and the wind in her hair with a huge smile on her face the whole way down the slope. It was magnificent.

There are some similarities to this scene and the ones Jesus painted in our passage this week. In the same way that the skiers had to know the voice of their instructor, the sheep had to know their shepherd's voice so well that they could pick his voice out of a cacophony of other voices. They had to tune in, listen, and follow that singular voice until they were safely out in the open spaces and green pastures.

But do you wonder how the sheep learned to recognize that one particular voice in the sea of so many others? Like the ski instructor teaching at the base of the mountain, the shepherd would go into the sheep pen every morning and talk to his sheep. He spent time with them in the safety of the pen before he led them out into the crowded streets. It was this time, when there was no confusion over which voice was speaking, that allowed the sheep to know and follow the right voice.

We have to spend time listening to the voice of our Savior in order to recognize the voice of our Savior. Our world is a noisy place. We hear the voices that preach a false gospel and the voices that minimize the true gospel. We hear self-help voices that say you will find your happiness from what is within you and social media influencers that say you will find your happiness from what is outside of you. These aren't the voices we should follow—they should cause us to flee because we know they are not the voice of our good shepherd. And the only way we will know that is by spending time listening to his voice. God has spoken to us through his word, and as we read, study, and obey, we are able to more easily recognize and follow his voice.

I want to be like those skiers. I want my life to be characterized by listening, knowing, and obeying. As I do, I know the joy of the Lord will be mine. As the sheep were taken out to green pastures, they frolicked, they played, they ate, and they were satisfied. They had abundant life. All because they followed their good shepherd.

Isaiah 30:21 says, "Your ears shall hear a word behind you, saying, 'This is the way, walk in it,' when you turn to the right or when you turn to the left." This is my hope for us all—that we will hear his voice, know his voice, follow his voice. And that we will all experience the joy of following him.

1. What are some practical ways you can grow in knowing the word of God? If you are new to the Bible, what's one barrier you are facing as you approach the Bible?

_____

_____

_____

_____

2. Describe a time you have felt the joy of obeying the voice of the Lord—or a time you struggled to obey.

_____

_____

_____

_____

🩶 Memory Verse

"[Jesus said,] 'I am the door. If anyone enters by me, he will be saved and will go in and out and find pasture.'" _John 10:9_

DISCUSSION QUESTIONS

Icebreaker: What's the prettiest door you have ever seen?

Warm-up: In two or three words, how are you most like a sheep?

1. Read John 10:1-10. Describe what a door is and does. How does this help you understand why Jesus called himself the door? Also, what does this passage teach about the thief? Why do we have to be so careful?

_____

_____

_____

2. Describe what you think Jesus meant (and what he didn't mean) when he said, "I came that they may have life and have it abundantly" (v. 10). Is he talking about eternal life, life here and now, both, or neither? Explain why.

3. Why is God's word the most important way to hear the voice of Jesus? How has time spent in God's word made you better able to quickly follow the voice of Jesus?

4. Read Psalm 118:19–22. In what ways is this prayer fulfilled in Jesus?

5. Why might Matthew 25:1–13 compel you to share the gospel with someone?

_____

_____

6. We know sheep can be lost, led astray, wounded, and at risk. What are examples of modern-day thieves that can lead us astray? We also know that sheep can be rescued, protected, safe, and provided for. How has God done these things for you?

_____

_____

_____

_____

7. What was one thing that stood out, convicted, encouraged, or instructed you this week?

_____

_____

_____

_____

8. How did this text help you see, believe, and live?

What did you see or learn about Jesus?

_____

_____

What do you need to believe as a result?

_____

_____

How should you live differently?

_____

_____

4

I Am the Good Shepherd

Welcome back! Last week we studied the first part of John 10, focusing on Jesus as the door to the sheep pen. This week we will still be in John 10, but we'll look at the fourth of Jesus's "I am" statements—"I am the good shepherd." If you recall, in the ancient Near East, sheep pens in rural areas didn't always have a gate or door. In those cases, the shepherd himself would lie down across the opening to keep the sheep in and harm out. So it's not difficult to understand why these two metaphors are in the same passage. The good shepherd loved his sheep by becoming the door.

We will see that good shepherds are those who care for, protect, and provide for their sheep. But Jesus is greater than even the best shepherd because he did so much more than simply care for his sheep—he died so his sheep can live.

Prayer for the Week

Father, thank you for sending your Son to save me. Help me to know his voice and follow where he leads. Teach me what it means that Jesus is my good shepherd. Meet me as I open your living word this week. In Jesus's name, Amen.

🩶 **Memory Verse:**

"I am the good shepherd. The good shepherd lays down his life for the sheep."
John 10:11

OBSERVATION
What Does the Text Say?

John 10:11–18

"I am the good shepherd. The good shepherd lays down his life for the sheep. He who is a hired hand and not a shepherd, who does not own the sheep, sees the wolf coming and leaves the sheep and flees, and the wolf snatches them and scatters them. He flees because he is a hired hand and cares nothing for the sheep. I am the good shepherd. I know my own and my own know me, just as the Father knows me and I know the Father; and I lay down my life for the sheep. And I have other sheep that are not of this fold. I must bring them also, and they will listen to my voice. So there will be one flock, one shepherd. For this reason the Father loves me, because I lay down my life that I may take it up again. No one takes it from me, but I lay it down of my own accord. I have authority to lay it down, and I have authority to take it up again. This charge I have received from my Father."

―――

If you remember from chapter 2, immediately after Jesus declared that he is the light of the world, he opened the eyes of a man who had been born blind. Jesus was showing that he is the one who brings both physical and spiritual sight and light to people. But after the miraculous healing, the religious leaders in Jerusalem were indignant at both Jesus's claim about himself and about the sign he used to substantiate his claim. The religious leaders didn't want the people to follow Jesus, so they cast the newly sighted man out of the synagogue as a means of warning anyone who was considering following Jesus. It was a manipulative scare tactic meant to dissuade the people. And with it, the tension between Jesus and the Jewish leaders increased.

This type of poor leadership is the backdrop for our passage this week. Throughout Scripture, as we'll see on Day 3, the leaders of God's people are referred to as shepherds (Ezek. 34:2) and God's people as sheep (Ezek. 34:31). In John 10, Jesus, the good shepherd, the one who takes care of his sheep, was warning the people that there were also bad shepherds in their midst—shepherds who didn't protect the sheep but misled them instead. Jesus wanted them to know that who they followed mattered. What a needed message for us today!

Read John 10:11-18 and answer the following questions.

1. What do you learn about each of the following?

Good shepherd:

_____

_____

Sheep:

_____

_____

Hired hand:

_____

_____

Wolf:

_____

_____

Father:

_____

_____

Sheep from other sheepfolds:

_____

_____

2. Briefly summarize in your own words what Jesus teaches in this passage.

_____

_____

_____

_____

3. Underline each time Jesus mentions laying down his life. Next to each verse reference below, write one thing you learn about Jesus laying down his life.

v. 11

_____

_____

v. 15

_____

_____

v. 17

_____

_____

v. 18

_____

_____

4. Why does the hired hand flee? What role does he play in the harm of the sheep?

_____

_____

_____

_____

5. What are the differences between the good shepherd and the hired hand? What is the result of each for the sheep?

Good Shepherd	Hired Hand

6. How well does Jesus know his sheep? To what does he compare this knowledge?

_____

_____

_____

_____

The word used for "know" in verses 14–15 means a lot more than simply intellectual information. It's a beautiful word used to describe one of the most intimate of all relationships—the intimacy shared between husband and wife. It indicates profound knowledge coupled with deep love and complete trust. Supremely, this is how the Father knows the Son and the Son knows the Father. Jesus was saying that this is also the way he knows us and we can know him. Incredible.

7. Where in this passage do you see evidence of the fact that Jesus is no mere man, but is, in fact, fully God?

_____

_____

_____

_____

8. From this passage, write down everything you learn about how Jesus's death will come about.

_____

_____

_____

_____

Wolves seek to kill and devour the sheep. Hired hands don't care about the sheep and leave them to die. But the good shepherd knows and loves his sheep—and will sacrifice himself so they will be safe. That's a shepherd worth following. My prayer for us this week is that we will learn to trust the good shepherd more and, as a result, follow wherever he leads.

💜 **Memory Verse:**

"I am the good shepherd. The good shepherd lays down his life for the sheep." *John 10:11*

INTERPRETATION
What Does the Text Mean?

Today we will begin to unpack the meaning of Jesus's words in John 10:11–18. This passage is full of gospel truths and practical realities for ways we are to live in light of the gospel. I'm excited to dig in together!

1. Remembering what you studied last week, imagine the scenario in verses 11–13. What are some reasons it might be important for the sheep to know the shepherd's voice?

_____

_____

_____

_____

2. What if Jesus had simply said, "I am the shepherd" instead of "I am the *good* shepherd"? Or if he had said, "I am *a* good shepherd" instead of "I am *the* good shepherd"? What difference would that make?

3. In verse 16, Jesus talked about sheep from other folds. Who might those sheep be? What does Jesus say about the flock? What do you think it might mean that Jesus has sheep from other folds but that there is just one flock?

4. As we saw earlier, to "know" means intimate knowledge and close relationship, not just awareness of. In the chart below, write down what "being known" might mean in each of these relationships.

The Father and the Son Know Each Other	Jesus Knows His Sheep	Jesus's Sheep Know Him

5. Consider the difference between a voluntary death and an involuntary one.

Why is it important that Jesus laid his own life down?

_____

_____

How does verse 18 show the divinity of Jesus?

_____

_____

Shepherds know there is danger in their profession. They can be wounded or possibly killed as they protect their sheep. But in this passage, Jesus makes clear that his approaching death was not an accidental ramification of his job. His death was voluntary and planned. The good shepherd was sent by his Father for the purpose of dying for his sheep.

6. Using the metaphor of sheep following either the good shepherd or a hired hand, describe how that might relate to you.

_____

_____

_____

_____

7. How do these verses increase your understanding of the gospel (the good news that Jesus came to die on the cross in order to save sinners)?

_____

_____

Spend some time today working on your memory verse and thinking about what it means for each of us. Jesus, the good shepherd, has come not only to call his sheep to himself, protect them, and lead them; he has come to lay down his life in order that they might live.

💜 Memory Verse

"I am the good shepherd. The good shepherd lays down his life for the sheep." *John 10:11*

INTERPRETATION
What Does the Whole Bible Say?

The Bible is one cohesive story, so tracing a theme (or an idea) throughout the story of Scripture is a beautiful and helpful way to study the Bible. One theme we can trace through the biblical narrative is that of shepherds. The first shepherd in the Bible's story is Abel, in Genesis 4. He is pictured as faithful and pleasing to the Lord. A lot of significant people in the Old Testament—Abraham, Rachel, Isaac, Jacob, Moses, Zipporah, David—were shepherds at one point in their lives. But let's work our way through the story, looking at different places in Scripture that develop this theme. We'll consider verses in chronological order so that we can better see how the idea of a shepherd for God's people progresses.

1. Read Numbers 27:16–19. Moses was the author of Numbers and the man God used to lead his people out of slavery in Egypt. What did he pray for in this passage? Why might it have been important for him to pray for someone to

shepherd God's people at this particular time? (This prayer was prayed at the end of his own life and his time of leading God's people and immediately before the new leader, Joshua, took over.)

_____

_____

_____

_____

2. Read Jeremiah 23:1–3. We again see a contrast between what bad shepherds do to the sheep and what God, as a good shepherd, will do. What similarities do you see with Jesus's words in John 10? How does God respond to poor shepherding?

_____

_____

_____

_____

3. Read Psalm 23. You might be familiar with this well-known psalm (it's the first Scripture I ever memorized!), but let's look carefully to see what we can learn about how God shepherds his people.

What is the first thing we learn about what it means that God is our shepherd (v. 1)?

_____

_____

What are the different things the Lord provides (vv. 2–3)?

_____

_____

Where are the different places the Lord leads (vv. 3–4)?

_____

_____

What is the final destination for those following this good shepherd? How long will they be there (v. 6)?

_____

_____

The shepherd of Psalm 23 led his sheep not only to places of peace and provision—green pastures, still waters—he also led his sheep into hard, even frightening places—the valley of the shadow of death. In the same way, Jesus, as our good shepherd, leads us both to places we love to go and places we'd rather never go. But he never stops being the good shepherd. He's good when the path you're on and the circumstances surrounding you are pleasant and peaceful, and Jesus is good when the path and the circumstances are rocky, dark, and frightening. In Psalm 23, the good shepherd never left his sheep, he never stopped loving them or protecting them, and he never stopped providing what they needed. We'll look more at this on Day 4, but today you can rest in humble confidence that our good shepherd is with you on every path. There is no path on which he will ever leave you or forsake you.

4. Read Ezekiel 34:1–10. What were the "shepherds" doing and what were they not doing?

What was the result for the sheep?

_____

_____

What was the result for the shepherds?

_____

_____

5. Read Ezekiel 34:11–16. List all the things the Lord says he will do. What similarities do you see to our passage in John 10? What similarities do you see to Psalm 23?

_____

_____

_____

_____

God was promising that he, himself, would be the shepherd for his people. He would be the one to rescue, gather, feed, and protect them. But in verse 23 of Ezekiel 34, God said, "I will set up over them one shepherd, my servant David, and he shall feed them: he shall feed them and be their shepherd." As the readers, we should be wondering, "So who will be the shepherd—God or David?" And we don't get the answer until John 10, when Jesus says that he himself is the good shepherd. How could the shepherd be both God himself as well as a man? Because Jesus is fully God and fully man, the greater David, the Son of God, sent to rescue his sheep.

6. Read Luke 15:1–7.

What is the response of the shepherd when he finds his lost sheep? How does he bring it home?

_____

_____

In reality, each one of us is either spiritually lost or found. How would you describe yourself spiritually today?

_____

_____

As we trace this theme to the end of the story, however, there is a plot twist for us.

7. Revelation 7:17. What shocking (and glorious) piece of the story do we learn? How does this help us better understand John 10? Where is the shepherd at the end of the story? Where is he leading his people and what will be done for them there?

_____

_____

_____

_____

Revelation is the last book of the Bible, and it describes a vision that the apostle John saw years after he wrote the Gospel we are studying. It describes events from a heavenly perspective and tells of things that have or will occur in the heavenly realm. And what we read is that the Lamb who was slain is the good shepherd. The good shepherd is the Lamb who was slain. This was why, when John the Baptist saw Jesus, he said, "Behold, the Lamb of God, who takes away the sin of the world!" (John 1:29, 36). This is why we also read in Revelation:

> "Worthy is the Lamb who was slain,
> to receive power and wealth and wisdom and might
> and honor and glory and blessing!"

And I heard every creature in heaven and on earth and under the earth and in the sea, and all that is in them, saying,

> "To him who sits on the throne and to the Lamb
> be blessing and honor and glory and might forever and ever!"
>   (Rev. 5:12–13)

God's people, all who put their trust in Jesus, will worship this Lamb, this good shepherd, for all eternity. Spend some time today doing just that. Worship the Lamb.

💜 Memory Verse

"I am the good shepherd. The good shepherd lays down his life for the sheep." *John 10:11*

APPLICATION: *How Do I Faithfully Respond?* You know by now that today is the day we ask, *How do I respond to the truths I've studied this week?* And we've seen so many beautiful truths this week. But I want us to focus in on two words that can help us respond faithfully—"know" and "follow."

First of all, Jesus wants you to know him. Intimately. He already knows you, top to bottom, inside and out, past and future. And he loves you. Knowing Jesus will help you to love him. And loving Jesus will help you to trust him. And trusting Jesus will help you to follow him—which is the faithful response of sheep to their good shepherd.

1. What are three practical steps you can take to know Jesus better?

_____

_____

_____

_____

2. What are three truths from this passage that help you love Jesus more?

_____

_____

_____

_____

3. Go back and reread Ezekiel 34:11–16.

Have you ever felt too lost for God to find you? What does it mean to you today that he will seek after you?

_____

_____

In what ways do you feel broken, injured, or weak today? In what ways can you turn to the Lord for healing and strength?

_____

_____

How does knowing these things increase your love of and trust in your good shepherd? Or, if you are not a follower of Jesus, which of these do you most need him to do?

_____

_____

Write a prayer either asking him to act in your life according to these verses or thanking him for all he has done.

_____

_____

4. Consider the words of Psalm 23.

Where is Jesus currently leading you? What comfort or help do you find?

_____

_____

Write down four to six words that might describe how a sheep follows a good shepherd (e.g., _willingly_).

_____

_____

As we said in the beginning of this chapter, Jesus was not only telling people that he is the good shepherd; he was also warning them that there were bad shepherds, hired hands, and wolves in their midst. The same is certainly true for us today.

5. According to what you've learned about the Jewish leaders in Jesus's day, what qualities in a religious leader should you flee from? See 2 Peter 2:1–3.

_____

_____

_____

_____

There is a huge difference between an imperfect human leader and the type of leader Jesus called a hired hand or a wolf. All leaders, even the most godly, will fail and frustrate us. That is not what Jesus was warning against. He was warning against someone who seeks his own good, his own reputation, his own comfort. Bad shepherds are harsh, impatient, selfish, rude, and harm their sheep. At the hint of danger, they run away and protect themselves. And, most importantly, bad shepherds deny the works of Jesus and don't want others to follow him.

Good shepherds (humanly speaking), even though they are imperfect and can be frustrating at times, are characterized by kindness, patience, and a willingness to suffer for their sheep. They don't run away when danger comes; they run to protect the sheep. And, most importantly, they continually encourage people to follow Jesus.

6. Think about what differentiates good shepherds from bad shepherds.

Consider your church leaders, social media influencers, friends, and mentors. Do you follow people who point you to Jesus?

_____

_____

How might the Lord be warning you against following the wrong person or people?

_____

_____

If your pastor or ministry leader is a good shepherd, write a prayer of thanksgiving for him (you might even consider sharing it with him). If you don't currently have a pastor, write a prayer asking the Lord to lead you to one who is a good shepherd.

_____

_____

Jesus, our good shepherd, can find you, rescue you, carry, protect, provide for, and comfort you—because he knows you, loves you, and cherishes you. Ultimately, he proved that he was the good shepherd by laying his life down for you. So if you want to know who to follow, follow the one who died for you.

7. In what ways did this "I am" statement help you learn about Jesus?

What does it mean that Jesus is the good shepherd?

_____

_____

How does Jesus ask you to respond?

_____

_____

What specific promise is associated with this "I am" statement?

_____

_____

 Memory Verse

"I am the good shepherd. The good shepherd lays down his life for the sheep."
John 10:11

REFLECTION

In our house, we watch a lot of war movies. They're not usually my first choice, but I want to hang out with my family, so I've seen almost every war movie you could imagine. One that many of you have probably seen is *Saving Private Ryan*. It's a tense, graphic, moving story about a platoon sent to save a young soldier in World War II.

The backstory is about a family with four sons, all sent overseas to fight in different parts of Europe. Three of the sons are killed in different battles, and as reports of their deaths come across the desk of a transcriptionist, she notices the shared last name and informs the commanding general. The merciful decision is made to rescue the fourth son, Private James Ryan, still overseas fighting, in order to spare his family the grief of losing all four sons.

Captain John Miller is tasked to lead a platoon of eight men on this great rescue mission to find and save Private Ryan. Most of the movie is spent watching the platoon move through enemy territory as they search for Ryan. Several of the soldiers in the platoon die in the mission and (spoiler alert) even Captain Miller is killed in the final battle to rescue the young soldier.

But the good news is that James Ryan is found and rescued. He lives. He goes home to his family. And he leads a full, good life all because someone was sent to save him.

If this were the end of the movie, we could say that we can see themes of the gospel and redemption throughout the movie. They're not hard to see. One person was trapped, lost, and without hope. He was destined to die. But someone was sent to save him. This person went into battle and ultimately gave his life so that Ryan could live. It sounds like the gospel!

We, like Private Ryan, are trapped in our sin and without hope. We are lost and need to be found. And without a rescue, death will have the final say in our lives. But Jesus was sent to find us. He fought a tremendous battle to rescue us, and he gave his life so that we can live.

But there is a scene in *Saving Private Ryan* that switches the whole story and makes it the opposite of the gospel. The final battle takes place over the course of several days in the small French town of Ramelle. At the end, Captain John Miller is mortally shot in the chest and as he lies dying on the ground, he beckons Ryan to lean in. As Ryan puts his ear near the dying man's mouth, Miller whispers, "Earn this . . . earn it." And then he dies.

Oh, the difference those few words make! For starters, Miller went into the battle begrudgingly; Jesus went willingly. Miller died accidentally; Jesus told us four times in our passage this week that he laid his life down willingly, intentionally, and voluntarily. Miller remained dead; Jesus had the authority to pick up the life he laid down and rise from the dead. And Jesus never, ever tells us to earn it. It's a gift that he tells us to receive.

The last scene of the movie shows Ryan standing at the foot of Miller's grave. He tearfully says over the tomb, "I've tried to live my life the best I could. I hope that was enough. I hope that at least in your eyes I've earned what all of you have done for me." And then he, clearly bearing a heavy burden, turns to his wife and says, "Tell me I've led a good life. Tell me I'm a good man."

That's tragic. But is that you? Are you, like Private Ryan, trying to live the best life you can in hopes of earning the love of God? Are you attempting to be a good-enough person in hopes of earning your salvation? Oh, friend, let me invite you to put that burden down. The love of God can't be earned but, instead, is lavishly poured out on us. Because Jesus, the good shepherd, laid down his life, willingly, out of love, for you, his precious sheep. Receive it and live.

1. In what ways might you try to earn your own salvation?

2. What difference does it make that Jesus laid his own life down for you?

💜 Memory Verse

"I am the good shepherd. The good shepherd lays down his life for the sheep."
John 10:11

DISCUSSION QUESTIONS

Icebreaker: What is your favorite war movie?

Warm-up: Who was the last person who protected you?

1. What were the differences between the good shepherd and the hired hand, and what was the result for the sheep?

2. What if Jesus had simply said, "I am the shepherd" instead of, "I am the *good* shepherd"? Or if he had said, "I am *a* good shepherd" instead of, "I am *the* good shepherd"? What difference would that make?

3. In verse 16, Jesus talked about sheep from other folds. Who might those sheep be? What does Jesus say about the flock?

4. Read 2 Peter 2:1–3. In what ways are false teachers like the hired hands? How can we recognize them, and what is the danger for us?

5. How do these verses increase your understanding of the gospel (the good news that Jesus came to die on the cross in order to save sinners)?

6. Thinking about what differentiates good shepherds from bad shepherds:

Do you follow people who point you to Jesus? (Consider what sources you go to for advice or wisdom.)

How might the Lord be warning you against following the wrong person or people?

_____

_____

7. What was one thing that stood out/convicted/encouraged/instructed you this week?

_____

_____

_____

8. How did this text help you see, believe, and live?

What did you see or learn about Jesus?

_____

_____

What do you need to believe as a result?

_____

_____

How should you live differently?

_____

_____

I Am the Resurrection and the Life

With each "I am" statement, we've become more acquainted with this fascinating man named Jesus. We've watched him perform amazing miracles and make declarations about himself indicating that he is God. He claimed to be the source of everlasting nourishment and the guiding light of hope and truth. He explained that he protects and provides for his own as the sheep gate and the good shepherd, even laying his life down for his sheep. Many saw his signs, heard his words, and believed that Jesus is the Messiah, the Son of God. Others weren't convinced, and many were enraged by his audacity. What about you? Do you find his case convincing, or are you skeptical? Do you think his words are life-giving or offensive?

The next passage we'll explore is different. You might want to dismiss Jesus's previous statements as misguided or delusional, and perhaps even attribute miracles like the feeding of the five thousand to some elaborate sleight of hand. However, Jesus's next miracle is much harder to rationalize. In this story, Jesus performs his final and greatest sign before his crucifixion that was in many ways the catalyst for Jesus's arrest, trial, and ultimately, death. This miracle not only precipitated Jesus's death, but it also pointed ahead to his resurrection, and one day, our resurrection as well. This week we'll consider what it means to have true life right now and the future Jesus offers after death.

Prayer for the Week

Dear God, thank you for giving your Son to die so that I can live. As I think about the uncomfortable reality of death, help me have hope in Jesus. Give me wisdom and understanding as I read your word this week. In Jesus's name, Amen.

Memory Verse

"Jesus said to her, 'I am the resurrection and the life. Whoever believes in me, though he die, yet shall he live, and everyone who lives and believes in me shall never die. Do you believe this?'" *John 11:25-26*

OBSERVATION
What Does the Text Say?

John 11:1–57

Now a certain man was ill, Lazarus of Bethany, the village of Mary and her sister Martha. It was Mary who anointed the Lord with ointment and wiped his feet with her hair, whose brother Lazarus was ill. So the sisters sent to him, saying, "Lord, he whom you love is ill." But when Jesus heard it he said, "This illness does not lead to death. It is for the glory of God, so that the Son of God may be glorified through it."

Now Jesus loved Martha and her sister and Lazarus. So, when he heard that Lazarus was ill, he stayed two days longer in the place where he was. Then after this he said to the disciples, "Let us go to Judea again." The disciples said to him, "Rabbi, the Jews were just now seeking to stone you, and are you going there again?" Jesus answered, "Are there not twelve hours in the day? If anyone walks in the day, he does not stumble, because he sees the light of this world. But if anyone walks in the night, he stumbles, because the light is not in him." After saying these things, he said to them, "Our friend Lazarus has fallen asleep, but I go to awaken him." The disciples said to him, "Lord, if he has fallen asleep, he will recover." Now Jesus had spoken of his death, but they thought that he meant taking rest in sleep. Then Jesus told them plainly, "Lazarus has died, and for your sake I am glad that I was not there, so that you may believe. But let us go to him." So Thomas, called the Twin, said to his fellow disciples, "Let us also go, that we may die with him."

Now when Jesus came, he found that Lazarus had already been in the tomb four days. Bethany was near Jerusalem, about two miles off, and many of the Jews had come to Martha and Mary to console them concerning their brother. So when Martha heard that Jesus was coming, she went and met him, but Mary remained seated in the house. Martha said to Jesus, "Lord, if you had been here, my brother would not have died. But even now I know that whatever you ask from God, God will give you." Jesus said to her, "Your brother will rise again." Martha said to him, "I know that he will rise again in the resurrection on the last day." Jesus said to her, "I am the resurrection and the life. Whoever believes in me, though he die, yet shall he live, and everyone who lives and believes in me shall never die. Do you believe this?" She said to him, "Yes, Lord; I believe that you are the Christ, the Son of God, who is coming into the world."

When she had said this, she went and called her sister Mary, saying in private, "The Teacher is here and is calling for you." And when she heard it, she rose quickly and went to him. Now Jesus had not yet come into the village, but was still in the place where Martha had met him. When the Jews who were with her in the house, consoling her, saw Mary rise quickly and go out, they followed her, supposing that she was going to the tomb to weep there. Now when Mary came to where Jesus was and saw him, she fell at his feet, saying to him, "Lord, if you had been here, my brother would not have died." When Jesus saw her weeping, and the Jews who had come with her also weeping, he was deeply moved in his spirit and greatly troubled. And he said, "Where have you laid him?" They said to him, "Lord, come and see." Jesus wept. So the Jews said, "See how he loved him!" But some of them said, "Could not he who opened the eyes of the blind man also have kept this man from dying?"

Then Jesus, deeply moved again, came to the tomb. It was a cave, and a stone lay against it. Jesus said, "Take away the stone." Martha, the sister of the dead man, said to him, "Lord, by this time there will be an odor, for he has been dead four days." Jesus said to her, "Did I not tell you that if you believed you would see the glory of God?" So they took away the stone. And Jesus lifted up his eyes and said, "Father, I thank you that you have heard me. I knew that you always hear me, but I said this on account of the people standing around, that they may believe that you sent me." When he had said these things, he cried out with a loud voice, "Lazarus, come out." The man who had died came out, his hands and feet bound with linen strips, and his face wrapped with a cloth. Jesus said to them, "Unbind him, and let him go."

Many of the Jews therefore, who had come with Mary and had seen what he did, believed in him, but some of them went to the Pharisees and told them what Jesus had done. So the chief priests and the Pharisees gathered the council and said, "What are we to do? For this man performs many signs. If we let him go on like this, everyone will believe in him, and the Romans will come and take away both our place and our nation." But one of them, Caiaphas, who was high priest that year, said to them, "You know nothing at all. Nor do you understand that it is better for you that one man should die for the people, not that the whole nation should perish." He did not say this of his own accord, but being high priest that year he prophesied that Jesus would die for the nation, and not for the nation only, but also to gather into one the children of God who are scattered abroad. So from that day on they made plans to put him to death.

Jesus therefore no longer walked openly among the Jews, but went from there to the region near the wilderness, to a town called Ephraim, and there he stayed with the disciples.

Now the Passover of the Jews was at hand, and many went up from the country to Jerusalem before the Passover to purify themselves. They were looking for Jesus and saying to one another as they stood in the temple, "What do you think? That he will not come to the feast at all?" Now the chief priests and the Pharisees had given orders that if anyone knew where he was, he should let them know, so that they might arrest him.

Today we'll begin working through an astonishing passage of Scripture. Up to this point we've seen Jesus perform miracles and make some bold claims about himself, but now we'll witness something even more amazing—Jesus overturning death. We'll start by observing details in the text to help us comprehend what it says. Begin with prayer, then read John 11 before answering the questions below.

1. Several themes run through this passage. Highlight or underline each of the following elements in a different color in the printed text. What connections do you notice between these themes?

   References to death (death, tomb, etc.):

   _____

   _____

   References to life (resurrection, awaken, etc.):

   _____

   _____

   References to believing:

   _____

   _____

2. What do we learn about Jesus's relationship with Mary, Martha, and Lazarus?

   _____

   _____

   _____

   _____

3. Instead of coming to Lazarus as soon as Jesus heard he was ill, Jesus waited. What was the purpose of Jesus's delay and Lazarus's illness and death according to the verses below?

v. 4

_____

_____

vv. 5–6

_____

_____

v. 15

_____

_____

4. In verses 25–27, Jesus declared his fifth "I am" statement to Martha.

What did Jesus call Martha to believe?

_____

_____

What is the result of believing?

_____

_____

What did Martha say she believed?

_____

_____

Do you think what Jesus called Martha to believe in verses 26 and 27 and what she said she believed in verse 28 are the same or different?

_____

_____

5. In the face of sickness or death, people respond in many ways. How did the people below respond to Lazarus's death, as well as to Jesus's delay and tears?

Martha (vv. 21–27):

_____

_____

Mary (vv. 32–33):

_____

_____

The Jews (vv. 19, 31, 33–37):

_____

_____

6. Jesus's interactions with Martha, Mary, and Lazarus show us a lot about how Jesus responds to grief and death. How did Jesus respond to each person?

Martha (vv. 21–27, 40):

_____

_____

Mary (vv. 32–35):

_____

_____

Lazarus (vv. 38–44):

_____

_____

7. Did any details in the story surprise you or confuse you? Do you have any questions about the passage?

_____

_____

_____

_____

Can you imagine what it must have been like to witness Jesus raising Lazarus from the dead? Imagine being in Mary or Martha's shoes—grieving the death of your brother and calling for help from the only one you know can save him, only to have him show up when it was too late. Imagine hearing the words "I am the resurrection and the life" as your brother lay lifeless in a tomb. What do you think you would have felt in that moment? Confusion? Disappointment? Anger? Hope? But from his words of hope, to his tears of grief, to his life-giving work, Jesus shows us that our circumstances don't change God's love for us and that he is always working in ways we could never imagine.

💜 Memory Verse

"Jesus said to her, 'I am the resurrection and the life. Whoever believes in me, though he die, yet shall he live, and everyone who lives and believes in me shall never die. Do you believe this?'" *John 11:25–26*

INTERPRETATION
What Does the Text Mean?

Now that we've had a chance to become familiar with what happened in the text, let's look a bit deeper at what the passage is communicating to us. Begin by praying for God to give you wisdom, and then read John 11 again before answering the questions below.

1. Our world characterizes death in a variety of ways. Some view it as an enemy to be overcome, while others welcome it as a friend. Some consider it ceasing to exist, while others believe in life after death. What do we learn about death from the way Jesus talked about and responded to death? (See vv. 4, 11–15, 23–27, 33–35, 38–44)

_____

_____

_____

_____

2. Jesus said in verse 4 that Lazarus's illness would not lead to death. How might you interpret this statement on a first reading? What do you think Jesus meant now that you've read the whole story?

_____

_____

_____

_____

3. Common superstition in the first century was that the spirit of a dead person hovered around the body for three days in case it was resuscitated, but left once decay set in. Why do you think Jesus waited until Lazarus was dead four days to resurrect him?

_____

_____

_____

_____

4. When Jesus told Martha, "I am the resurrection and the life. Whoever believes in me, though he die, yet shall he live, and everyone who lives and believes in me shall never die. Do you believe this?" (vv. 25–26), Martha responded yes, but rather than repeating Jesus's statement, she said, "I believe that you are the Christ, the Son of God, who is coming into the world" (v. 27). Initially, her statement may not seem to align with Jesus's question. Now consider the purpose of the Gospel of John: "These are written so that you may believe that Jesus is the Christ, the Son of God, and that by believing you may have life in his name" (20:31). How does this verse help you interpret Martha's response to Jesus?

_____

_____

5. What do you think is the difference between Jesus's claim to be "the resurrection" and his claim to be "the life" in verse 25? How do the rest of verses 25 and 26 inform your response? See also Ephesians 2:1-7.

6. How does Jesus's statement that he is the resurrection and the life offer hope that surpasses Martha's belief in resurrection on the last day?

7. When we seek God's help, we often have ideas of how God should act, and we long for God to answer our prayers accordingly. Yet God often works in ways different than we anticipate. When Martha and Mary sent word to Jesus that Lazarus was ill, what outcome do you think they hoped for? What was the outcome of Jesus's response? How does that outcome differ from what they hoped for? (See vv. 4, 15, 25-27, 35-37, 40, 43-45, 49-53)

Death is a topic many of us try to avoid, perhaps because it stirs up fear, grief, or the anxiety of unanswered questions or feeling out of control. But Jesus confronted death boldly. He viewed it as an enemy worthy of our sorrow and tears, but he also proclaimed with his words and actions that death does not have the final word. In fact, Jesus is the resurrection and the life that defeats death. As we continue to study Jesus's fifth "I am" statement, we'll see how Jesus solves this problem, not only for Lazarus, but for all who believe in him.

♡ Memory Verse

"Jesus said to her, 'I am the resurrection and the life. Whoever believes in me, though he die, yet shall he live, and everyone who lives and believes in me shall never die. Do you believe this?'" *John 11:25–26*

INTERPRETATION
What Does the Whole Bible Say?

The account of Jesus raising Lazarus from the dead is a remarkable story of hope and life when death seems final. However, does Lazarus's resurrection solve the problem of illness and death we all still face? After all, we don't witness Jesus resurrecting dead bodies now. Today we'll look at other parts of Scripture to help us understand what Jesus meant when he said life is available to us now and resurrection is coming. Start your study by praying for God to give you understanding and faith as you read, then read John 11 again before moving on to the questions below.

1. When Jesus told Martha that her brother would rise again, she acknowledged that he would rise again in the resurrection on the last day. Many Jews believed in future resurrection, and Jesus taught that it was true. What do each of the following passages tell you about the future resurrection?

   Daniel 12:1–3:

   _____

   _____

   John 5:28:

   _____

   _____

   Philippians 3:20–21:

   _____

   _____

   Revelation 21:1–8:

   _____

   _____

2. Raising Lazarus from the dead was one of the major events that led to Jesus's death, but it also pointed ahead to what would happen after Jesus was crucified. Read John 20:1–18. What similarities do you see between Lazarus's resurrection and Jesus's resurrection?

   _____

   _____

_____

_____

Jesus showed Mary that her belief in the resurrection wasn't belief just in an idea, but in a person—*Jesus* is the resurrection and the life. The resurrection of Jesus is a central doctrine of the Christian faith, not simply because it is a miraculous event, but because it accomplishes something for everyone who trusts in Jesus. Let's take a closer look at the impact of Jesus's resurrection on believers.

3. Lazarus's resurrection pointed to Jesus's resurrection, and Jesus's resurrection points to something else. Read 1 Corinthians 15:20-23. What does Jesus's resurrection anticipate?

_____

_____

_____

_____

4. The Bible shows us that people who believe in Jesus are united to him. Jesus described this union as believers being in him and he in believers (John 14:20). If you are united to Jesus, then everything he accomplishes counts for you. What do each of the passages below tell you about what Jesus accomplishes for everyone who believes in him?

Romans 6:3–5:

_____

_____

Galatians 2:20:

_____

_____

We all face the same problem—death. All of us sin and rebel against God and have earned the same consequence for our actions. Romans 6:23 says, "The wages of sin is death, but the free gift of God is eternal life in Christ Jesus our Lord." If we trust in Jesus, his death counts as the punishment for our sin, and his resurrection means we have new life in him. We've already seen that Jesus's resurrection means that our bodies will one day be raised back to life like his, but Jesus also promised life now. Let's look at what it means to experience resurrection life today.

5. In Romans 6, Paul explains that when we believe in Jesus, his death and resurrection give us new life right now. Without Jesus, our sin made us enemies of God who were condemned to death. But when we trust in Jesus, the person we used to be dies with him, and we are raised to new spiritual life. When we have new life, it changes the way we go about our days. Read Romans 6:6–14.

    From what does Christ's death free believers (vv. 6–7)?

    _____

    _____

    What does Christ's resurrection accomplish for believers (vv. 9–11)?

    _____

    _____

    How does Christ's death and resurrection impact a believer's life now (vv. 12–14)?

    _____

    _____

Have you ever had an impulse so strong that you felt hopeless to resist it? Without Jesus, sin has the power to control us and destroy our lives, but Jesus's death and resurrection frees us from our slavery to sin. Because of Jesus, we have a new power to live the way God calls us to live, and that's the best thing for us. We don't obey God's commands to earn eternal life—eternal life is a gift from God for those who have faith in Jesus. But when we believe in Jesus, he gives us new spiritual life and the power to obey that we didn't have before. Let's see what it looks like to walk in the new life we've received.

6. Read Colossians 3:1–17. Make a list of what believers are called to put to death (what they should stop doing) and another of what believers are to put on (what they should do). How are those commands connected to Jesus's death and resurrection?

Put to Death	Put On

7. Even though we can have spiritual life now, we still experience physical death and sickness. Read 1 Peter 1:3–9, 13.

How does Peter describe the inheritance for those who are born again? How does that differ from our lives now?

How does the future hope of resurrection impact the way we experience suffering?

_____

_____

When Jesus said he is the resurrection and the life, he was offering hope for all who believe in him. Life isn't something we can achieve, and resurrection isn't just a doctrine we affirm. Jesus *is* the resurrection and the life, and it's through relationship with him that we experience the same.

💜 Memory Verse

"Jesus said to her, 'I am the resurrection and the life. Whoever believes in me, though he die, yet shall he live, and everyone who lives and believes in me shall never die. Do you believe this?'" *John 11:25-26*

APPLICATION: *How Do I Faithfully Respond?* Jesus promised a solution to everyone's biggest problem—death. Today, we'll consider how we can respond to Jesus's claim and enjoy the blessings of that promise even today. Pray and ask God to help you clearly see your own heart. Then read John 11 again and answer the questions below.

1. What is your reaction to talking about death? Is it something you try to avoid? Are you afraid of death? How does this week's text challenge the way you view death?

_____

_____

_____

2. Imagine Jesus asked you the same question he asked Martha in John 11:25–26, when he said, "I am the resurrection and the life. Whoever believes in me, though he die, yet shall he live, and everyone who lives and believes in me shall never die. Do you believe this?" How would you honestly answer that question? Do you have any questions or hesitations about his claim?

When we believe in Jesus, we not only have the future hope of resurrection; we also have new life now. Jesus doesn't just forgive us and give us a ticket to heaven; he transforms us right now.

3. Look back at the lists you made yesterday from Colossians 3:1–17. What do you most struggle to "put to death"? What do you most need to "put on"?

Jesus promised life now and for eternity, but we still experience difficult things. These two realities can feel hard to reconcile, but Jesus teaches us how to navigate the pain of this world while we wait to see death defeated.

4. Are there any circumstances in your life that lead you to doubt God's love? How do you respond to God when it seems like his help is delayed? How does the story of Lazarus shape the way you respond?

5. Consider the way Jesus responded to death and his interactions with Martha, Mary, and Lazarus. How might these interactions impact the way you care for someone who is grieving?

6. How are the problems of illness and death impacting you right now? How does the future resurrection encourage you? What are some practical things you can do to remind yourself of that future hope?

Jesus offers the greatest solution to our biggest problem—death. If his claims are true, we can have hope that would otherwise be impossible.

7. In what ways did this "I am" statement help you learn about Jesus?

What does it mean that Jesus is the resurrection and the life?

How does Jesus ask you to respond?

What specific promise is associated with this "I am" statement?

 Memory Verse

"Jesus said to her, 'I am the resurrection and the life. Whoever believes in me, though he die, yet shall he live, and everyone who lives and believes in me shall never die. Do you believe this?'" *John 11:25–26*

REFLECTION

"Do what makes you feel alive."
"We only regret the chances we didn't take."
"Life is too short to be unhappy."
"You are your only limit."
"Carpe diem."

Have you ever heard statements like these? Perhaps you've seen these words of advice proclaimed on social media posts and coffee mugs as an exhortation to take advantage of the days you've been given before it's too late. Something in us knows that to truly live is more than just air in our lungs and blood pumping through our veins. And many of us suspect we're not experiencing life to the full.

The answer to our lifelessness isn't chasing an emotional high or packing our lives full of things that make us feel alive even if only for a moment. Instead, Jesus said the source of life is himself. "I am the resurrection and the life," Jesus says. "Whoever believes in me, though he die, yet shall he live, and everyone who lives and believes in me shall never die" (John 11:25–26). The life Jesus provides is unsurpassable and unbreakable. Christ offers the promise of life after death, the experience of everlasting life now, and comforting hope as we wait for sickness and death to come to an end.

Jesus is the resurrection. Death is an intruder, and for some who've seen tragedy strike those closest to them, it's a reality that shapes every moment of their days. Others go through life as if death were an illusion, living each day as if tomorrow is guaranteed. Still others see death as a welcome friend, a longed-for relief from the pain of the world. John 11 is a poignant reminder that death is the enemy. When Jesus called, "Lazarus, come out," he proved that death, as pernicious and powerful as it is, does not have the last word. In the greatest of all plot twists, Christ defeated death by dying. He took our place and paid the price for our sins when he bled and died. And then, three days later, he too rose to life, this time never to die again. And the promise for all who believe in him is this—though we die, yet we will live. Our bodies will be raised like his—imperishable, unfading, glorious. Our hope of life after death isn't in living a good life. We will be resurrected because he is the resurrection.

Jesus is also the life. New life doesn't begin after we die; it begins when we trust in Jesus. No longer are we spiritually dead, separated from God, and enslaved to sin. In Christ, we are alive to God, reconciled to him, and freed to walk in new life. So what does resurrection life look like now? It looks like living from a place of security instead of self-doubt, knowing that we are loved, forgiven, and purified, not because of anything we've done, but because Christ gave his life for ours. It looks like living with purpose, joyfully following God's commands even when they're difficult because we know that the one who gave his only Son for us wants what's best for us. It looks like living from hope, not fear, as we endure the suffering and grief that come from living in a broken world, confident in the knowledge that in Jesus, nothing can separate us from God's love. Not even death (Rom. 8:38–39).

For now, we still experience sickness and grief—death is all around us. But as the resurrection and the life, Jesus comforts us and causes us to persevere. We can set our hope, not on our present circumstances, but on the future reality that death will be no more. Death is the last enemy, and it will be defeated (1 Cor. 15:26). In the meantime, we experience decay and physical death, but those who are alive in Christ can never truly die.

You don't have to spend your years chasing things that make you *feel* alive; you can trust in the one who truly *makes* you alive. There is more to life than a beating heart, and you can experience it now.

1. Is Jesus as the resurrection and the life a source of hope for you today? Why or why not?

2. Read 2 Corinthians 4:16–18. Do you feel like you are "losing heart" today? What feels especially heavy? How practically can you take comfort in the hope of resurrection today?

💚 Memory Verse

"Jesus said to her, 'I am the resurrection and the life. Whoever believes in me, though he die, yet shall he live, and everyone who lives and believes in me shall never die. Do you believe this?'" *John 11:25-26*

DISCUSSION QUESTIONS

Icebreaker: What's your favorite (or perhaps least favorite) inspirational saying?

Warm-up: When was the last time you were frustrated because you had to wait on someone for something important?

1. Read John 11:21–27. What does it mean that Jesus is the resurrection and the life? How does that identity impact believers now and in the future?

2. Jesus said Lazarus's death was for the glory of God. How did Lazarus's death glorify God? What did it reveal about Jesus?

3. What are some different ways the world characterizes death? How do you tend to view death? How does Jesus's response to death transform the way you view it?

4. When Jesus let Lazarus die, some thought Jesus should have come sooner to heal him, but Jesus had plans to do something much greater. Share a time when your circumstances made it seem like God forgot you or abandoned you. Did you see God using it for good, or does it still feel unresolved?

5. What are you praying for God to do in your life right now? How do you expect God to answer your prayer? What might it look like for you to submit the answer to him?

6. Read Colossians 3:1–17. What does it mean to be alive in Christ today? How does resurrection power work in us today, allowing us to live in newness of life?

_____

_____

_____

7. How did this text help you see, believe, and live?

What did you see or learn about Jesus?

_____

_____

What do you need to believe as a result?

_____

_____

How should you live in response?

_____

_____

8. What was one thing that encouraged, convicted, or instructed you this week?

_____

_____

_____

6

I Am the Way, and the Truth, and the Life

We've seen and heard some remarkable things as we've walked through Jesus's life and ministry. He claimed to be the source of life and light, all while feeding the hungry, raising the dead, and even saying he would lay down his own life for his precious sheep. John spent the first half of his Gospel telling us who Jesus is and proving his claims with miraculous signs. Now we find ourselves in the second half, where we see Jesus's ultimate sign—the miracle of miracles. Every "I am" statement has been leading up to Jesus's death and resurrection, and now we join Jesus and his disciples just prior to that day—the day he was crucified.

At the end of John 13, Jesus gave his disciples some disheartening news: one of the twelve disciples would betray him, Jesus would leave to go to a place where they couldn't follow, and Peter would disown Jesus, not once but three times. The disciples didn't understand what was coming, and they were filled with confusion, sorrow, and fear. Jesus was troubled about the suffering he was about to endure, yet he encouraged his frightened disciples. As we encounter Jesus in this passage, we will see that comfort and hope are found in believing Jesus is the way, the truth, and the life.

Prayer for the Week

Father, thank you for providing a way to you, showing me the truth of who you are in Jesus, and offering me life through him. Show me more of Jesus and more of you. Help me clearly see the way I should go. In Jesus's name, Amen.

 Memory Verse

"Jesus said to him, 'I am the way, and the truth, and the life. No one comes to the Father except through me.'" *John 14:6*

OBSERVATION
What Does the Text Say?

John 14:1-11

"Let not your hearts be troubled. Believe in God; believe also in me. In my Father's house are many rooms. If it were not so, would I have told you that I go to prepare a place for you? And if I go and prepare a place for you, I will come again and will take you to myself, that where I am you may be also. And you know the way to where I am going." Thomas said to him, "Lord, we do not know where you are going. How can we know the way?" Jesus said to him, "I am the way, and the truth, and the life. No one comes to the Father except through me. If you had known me, you would have known my Father also. From now on you do know him and have seen him."

Philip said to him, "Lord, show us the Father, and it is enough for us." Jesus said to him, "Have I been with you so long, and you still do not know me, Philip? Whoever has seen me has seen the Father. How can you say, 'Show us the Father'? Do you not believe that I am in the Father and the Father is in me? The words that I say to you I do not speak on my own authority, but the Father who dwells in me does his works. Believe me that I am in the Father and the Father is in me, or else believe on account of the works themselves."

———

Have you ever received troubling news that left you anxious and discouraged for the future? Today we find the disciples frightened and confused about what the days ahead hold. Jesus told them he was leaving and that some of them would betray or deny him, and so they were asking Jesus questions that he didn't answer in the way they expected. Jesus offered them hope beyond their immediate circumstances, and that hope is for us too.

Read John 14:1–11 carefully, paying attention to details, and then answer the questions below.

1. Repeated words often reveal important emphases in the text. How many times does the word "Father" appear in these verses? What do you learn about the Father?

2. Look at verse 1. What does Jesus tell his disciples not to do? What does he tell them to do instead?

3. This passage begins and ends with commands to believe. What does Jesus call his disciples to believe in verses 1, 10, and 11?

4. The disciples were troubled about Jesus saying he would leave them. According to verses 2 and 3, what is Jesus's reason for leaving? What is his reason for coming back?

5. Jesus uses the metaphor of a house to describe God's dwelling place. What do we learn about the Father's house?

How much space is available in the Father's house?

Who are the "rooms" intended for?

Who will take the disciples to this house?

_____

_____

6. What three things does Jesus claim to be in verse 6? Which of these most directly answers Thomas's question from verse 5?

_____

_____

_____

_____

7. According to verse 8, what does Philip seem to desire above all else?

_____

_____

_____

_____

8. Do you have any questions about the text? Did any details of the story or of Jesus's responses to his disciples surprise or confuse you?

_____

_____

_____

_____

Jesus's disciples were afraid and troubled based on what they could see before Jesus's death and resurrection, but Jesus called them to look beyond the difficulties at hand to see the hope that is coming. As you go about your day, make note of the times you find yourself anxious or troubled about something challenging in your life, and consider how Jesus's words might be comforting. As we continue to explore this passage, it's my prayer that Jesus as the way, the truth, and the life will provide comfort even in our sorrow.

🩶 Memory Verse

"Jesus said to him, 'I am the way, and the truth, and the life. No one comes to the Father except through me. '" *John 14:6*

INTERPRETATION
What Does the Text Mean?

Today we'll look more closely at Jesus's words to his troubled and confused disciples to determine what they mean. Pray for God to guide you as you study, then read John 14:1–11 and answer the questions below.

Jesus saw that his disciples were distressed, and he encouraged them by urging them to believe in him and by talking about his Father's house. Many commentators agree that the Father's house is a metaphor for God's dwelling place, and that Jesus's promise to come again and take his disciples to himself refers to Christ's second coming. When Jesus comes back, everyone who believes in him will be resurrected to live in God's presence in a new creation where there will be no more suffering or sin or pain (Rev. 21). The "many rooms" communicate that there is ample space in God's presence for all who believe in Jesus.

Jesus explained where he was going and why, but the responses from the disciples revealed that they didn't understand. Jesus's words can be confusing for us too, so let's take a closer look at what they mean.

1. Jesus told the disciples where he was going, but Thomas told Jesus they didn't know where he was going. Look at what Jesus said in verse 1–4, as well as his statement in verse 6. Based on these verses, where do you think Jesus was going? How is it different than Thomas expected?

2. When Jesus told Thomas he knew the way to where Jesus was going, Thomas objected that he didn't know where Jesus was going, likely thinking Jesus was talking about a physical location. Based on verse 6, what do you think Jesus meant when he said, "You know the way" (v. 4)?

Does Jesus's claim to be the way, the truth, and the life remind you of anything he's said already? John spent the first thirteen chapters of his Gospel showing us who Jesus is and how he proved his "I am" statements through various miraculous signs. Now this claim summarizes all of Jesus's "I am" statements such that each one fits into one of these three categories.

3. Look back at the statements you've studied so far and place each one in the appropriate column in the chart below.

I am the bread of life (6:35)

I am the light of the world (8:12)

I am the door (10:7–9)

I am the good shepherd (10:11, 14)

I am the resurrection and the life (11:25)

The Way	The Truth	The Life

4. How does your past study of the statements in the chart help you understand what Jesus may have meant when he said, "I am the way, and the truth, and the life" (v. 6)?

5. In verse 6, Jesus further explains his claim to be the way, the truth, and the life by saying, "No one comes to the Father except through me." How would you expect a roomful of people to react to that statement today? What are some different "ways" people try to come to God?

The word "Father" appears eleven times in these eleven verses. Jesus called God his Father, so every time you see the word "Father," the passage is talking about God. Let's explore why the Father is so important in this passage.

6. Look back at the occurrences of "Father" you found in the text on Day 1. What do you think Jesus was claiming about himself and his relationship to the Father?

7. In verse 8, Philip asked Jesus to show him the Father. How did Philip misunderstand Jesus's statement in verse 7? What does Jesus's response show you about how someone can see and know the Father?

8. Based on your answers to the questions above, what is Jesus telling his disciples to believe when he says, "Believe in God; believe also in me" in verse 1? When properly understood, how is believing in Jesus a remedy for a troubled heart (v. 1)?

_____

_____

_____

_____

Many paths and religions promise life, joy, or relationship with God, but Jesus boldly claimed that he is the only way. He is the way to God because he reveals the truth about who God is and gives us life from God when we trust in him. As you think back on all you've learned about Jesus so far, consider what path you've chosen and whether you believe Jesus is the only way, as he claimed to be.

💙 **Memory Verse**

"Jesus said to him, 'I am the way, and the truth, and the life. No one comes to the Father except through me.'" *John 14:6*

INTERPRETATION
What Does the Whole Bible Say?

Jesus claimed to be the only way to the Father, and today we'll look at other parts of the Bible to understand why access to God is restricted, why finding a way to the Father is worthwhile, and how Jesus is the way. Begin in prayer before reading John 14:1–11, then answer the questions below.

Philip desperately wanted to see the Father, and Jesus declared that he is the only way to the Father, so let's explore why the Father's presence is something worth longing for.

1. What do each of the passages below tell you about knowing God, seeing God, or being in God's presence?

Psalm 16:11:

_____

_____

Psalm 27:4:

_____

_____

Psalm 84:10–12:

_____

_____

Revelation 21:1–4:

_____

_____

God's presence is the greatest good we can ever experience, but our access to God is restricted. God is perfectly holy, and we are not. As sinners, we can't come into the presence of God. In the Old Testament, God told his people to build a tabernacle, which was an elaborate tent, to be God's dwelling place among them. In the tabernacle, and later in the temple, there was a room called the Most Holy Place, or the Holy of Holies, which represented the place where God's presence dwelt.

2. Exodus 26:33 says, "You shall hang the veil from the clasps, and bring the ark of the testimony in there within the veil. And the veil shall separate for you the Holy Place from the Most Holy." What was the purpose of the veil hung in the tabernacle? What do you think that veil tells us about people's access to God?

_____

_____

_____

_____

The Most Holy Place was separated by a curtain 60 feet high and 30 feet wide, and nobody was allowed inside the Most Holy Place except the high priest, who could only enter once a year to make a sacrifice for the sins of God's people. Their sin separated them from God's presence, and so God appointed a priest to offer sacrifices on their behalf so they could have access to God.

In John 14, Jesus claimed that we can now have access to God through him. Many commentators agree that when Jesus said he was going to prepare a place for his disciples, he didn't mean that God's dwelling place was not ready for them, but that he needed to prepare the way for them to get there. Let's see how Jesus prepared himself as the way to the Father.

3. Matthew 27 recounts Jesus's death on the cross. Read verses 50 and 51. What happened to the curtain in the temple when Jesus died? What do you think this event signifies?

_____

_____

_____

_____

The book of Hebrews explains why the veil tearing when Jesus died is so significant. Let's look at a few verses that can help us understand how this event is connected to Jesus's claim to be the way to the Father.

4. Hebrews 9:12 says, "[Jesus] entered once for all into the holy places, not by means of the blood of goats and calves but by means of his own blood, thus securing an eternal redemption."

   How is Jesus better than the priests who made sacrifices in the Most Holy Place?

   How does Jesus as the better high priest help you better understand his claim to be "the way"?

   _____

   _____

5. Read Hebrews 10:19–22.

   Why can we have confidence to enter the holy places?

   _____

   _____

   How did Jesus open "the new and living way?"

   _____

   _____

Jesus made a way to the Father through his death on the cross, and anyone who believes in Jesus has access to God and will one day live in his presence forever.

6. Jesus proved his "I am" statements through various miracles and signs such as feeding five thousand people and healing the man born blind. In what ways do Jesus's death and resurrection serve as proof for his claim to be the way, the truth, and the life?

_____

_____

_____

_____

💜 **Memory Verse**

"Jesus said to him, 'I am the way, and the truth, and the life. No one comes to the Father except through me.'" *John 14:6*

APPLICATION: *How Do I Faithfully Respond?* The words of Jesus offered hope and encouragement to Jesus's disciples, and they can do the same for us now. Begin by praying for God to give you wisdom as you respond. Then read John 14:1–11 before answering the questions below.

1. John spent half his Gospel telling us who Jesus is by showing us his three years of earthly ministry, and the entire second half focuses on just the four days surrounding his death and resurrection. This structure points to Jesus's resurrection as the ultimate sign that proves he is everything he claimed to be. How does Jesus's resurrection impact the way you view Jesus? How will

you respond to his claim to be the way, the truth, and the life, considering the resurrection?

2. Jesus encouraged his disciples not to be troubled, but to believe in him. What specific circumstances or fears are causing your heart to be troubled right now? How might believing that Jesus is the way, the truth, and the life give you encouragement for your present and future?

3. What was your initial reaction to Jesus's claim to be the only way to God? Did you find it comforting, offensive, or something else? Has your perspective changed as you've studied?

4. Philip desperately wanted to see God, and the psalms we read on Day 3 reflect the desire to know God and live in his presence. Think about your own desires and life choices. Is knowing God the greatest desire of your heart right now? What other desires overshadow your hunger for God? What are some practical ways you can draw near to God through Jesus this week?

5. Jesus's disciples were troubled because he was leaving, and later they despaired at his death, but Jesus was crucified in order to be our way to God. Have you ever felt as if God abandoned you? How can Jesus's encouragement to his disciples give you encouragement when it seems like God is absent? Read Romans 8:31–32. How do these verses encourage you today?

6. Jesus's claim to be the only way to God is a reminder that apart from Jesus, our sin restricts our access to God. We can't make our own way to God, so Jesus became the way by dying on the cross for our sins. When we trust in Jesus, we are completely forgiven and have unrestricted access to God, but our sin can cause us to pull away and hinder our enjoyment of God's presence. Spend some time in prayer asking the Holy Spirit to bring your sins to mind and confessing the sins you see in your heart right now.

7. In what ways did this "I am" statement help you learn about Jesus?

What does it mean that Jesus is the way, the truth, and the life?

_____

_____

How does Jesus ask you to respond?

_____

_____

What specific promise is associated with this "I am" statement?

_____

_____

💙 Memory Verse

"Jesus said to him, 'I am the way, and the truth, and the life. No one comes to the Father except through me.'" *John 14:6*

REFLECTION

From my house, there are multiple ways to get to church or the grocery store or wherever we may be going. We're nestled between two exits on the interstate, and there are numerous back roads we can take instead. The way we go depends largely on who is driving. My husband chooses the route with the least left turns and the most time on the highway, while I prefer the shortest distance, even if it means an extra stop sign or two. It leads to never-ending, playful banter over which way is best. But when we reach our destination, the route makes almost no difference at all.

Many people view life much like my trips to the grocery store. Argue all you want about which way is best, but we'll all end up at the same place anyway. But Jesus opposed this notion with his exclusive claim that no one comes to the Father except through him.

Jesus is the way. He's the only path to the Father because only he gave his life to pay for our sins. We can't make our way to God by being kind or doing good things, because our sin means we can never do or be enough on our own. No other religion can be our path to God because no other god came down to us to make a way. Jesus graciously opened the door for us to enter in by becoming the door. Jesus is the way *because* he is the truth and the life.

Jesus is the truth. He shows us what God is like because he is God. Hebrews 1:3 says, "He is the radiance of the glory of God and the exact imprint of his nature." We can come to the Father through him because he is one with the Father. He told the truth about our sin and our need for him, and like a lamp for our feet, he lights the way to salvation. He is the truth that sets us free.

Jesus is the life. The life of God is found in him, and he imparts everlasting nourishment to all who feed on him. He laid his life down for his sheep, and his resurrection means all who believe in him will be resurrected too. Because he lived a sinless life, we can live in the freedom of obedience. He offers a life of purpose, abundance, and joy in knowing him. Jesus is the life because he gave his life for ours.

Without Jesus, there would be no way to God. Some find this statement offensive, but Jesus presented it as comfort and hope for troubled hearts. The only one who could make a way *did*, even though it came at the greatest cost. There is forgiveness for your past, help for your present, and hope for your future—all in the blood of Jesus. He isn't the best way, the shortest way, or the way with the least left turns—he is the only way.

1. If you believe in Jesus, how does his claim to be the only way to the Father spur you on to share your faith with others? If you are unsure about Jesus, how does this claim lead you to examine your own path in life?

_____

_____

_____

_____

2. Can you think of a time in your life when understanding Jesus as the way, the truth, and the life was or could have been particularly encouraging?

_____

_____

_____

_____

💜 **Memory Verse**

"Jesus said to him, 'I am the way, and the truth, and the life. No one comes to the Father except through me." _John 14:6_

DISCUSSION QUESTIONS

Icebreaker: What's your dream car?

Warm-up: When was the last time you had a disagreement over the best way to go somewhere or do something?

1. Look back at the chart you completed on Day 2 of this chapter. How did you categorize each "I am" statement and why?

_____

_____

2. What did Jesus mean when he said, "I am the way, and the truth, and the life"? How do this week's passage, Jesus's previous "I am" statements, and verses from the Old Testament help you reach that understanding?

3. Do you agree with Jesus's claim to be the only way to the Father? Why or why not?

4. Is there anything that is troubling you right now that we can pray for? What truth from Jesus's teaching this week can give you hope in that circumstance?

5. How would you describe your relationship with God? Is there anything that keeps you from drawing near to him through Jesus?

_____

_____

_____

6. What are some practical steps you can take to seek to know God better this week?

_____

_____

_____

_____

7. How did this text help you see, believe, and live?

What did you see or learn about Jesus?

_____

_____

What do you need to believe as a result?

_____

_____

How should you live in response?

_____

_____

8. What was one thing that encouraged, convicted, or instructed you this week?

7

I Am the True Vine

When my children were young, I went on a two-week trip overseas. Before I left, I made sure to leave detailed instructions. I tried to prepare the kids as much as possible for what those two weeks would be like. I reminded them of my love and my return. And I told them what to do when they were sad or scared. I knew it wouldn't be easy on them, and I wanted them to be prepared.

In our passage this week, Jesus did something similar. He prepared his disciples for his departure and gave them instruction on how they were to live as they waited for him to return. The words in our passage were spoken on a Thursday night, just hours before Jesus was arrested and crucified. He was walking from the upper room, where he had shared a meal with his disciples, to the garden of Gethsemane, where he cried out to God and sweated drops of blood in agony over what lay in front of him.

On that night, Jesus knew his disciples needed to be strengthened and encouraged (to have courage instilled in them) for two reasons. His imminent death would leave them feeling abandoned and afraid. But after his resurrection, he would return to his Father, and his disciples would also need to know how to live out their faith and carry forward the mission of God. So what did he tell them? "I am the true vine. . . . Abide in me."

Prayer for the Week

Father, thank you that you never leave us alone. You have sent both your Son and your Spirit to save, strengthen, comfort, and instruct us. I pray that you will anchor me more in the true vine, Jesus, and that you will bear much fruit in me through him. In Jesus's name, Amen.

Memory Verse

"I am the vine; you are the branches. Whoever abides in me and I in him, he it is that bears much fruit, for apart from me you can do nothing." *John 15:5*

OBSERVATION
What Does the Text Say?

John 15:1–17
"I am the true vine, and my Father is the vinedresser. Every branch in me that does not bear fruit he takes away, and every branch that does bear fruit he prunes, that it may bear more fruit. Already you are clean because of the word that I have spoken to you. Abide in me, and I in you. As the branch cannot bear fruit by itself, unless it abides in the vine, neither can you, unless you abide in me. I am the vine; you are the branches. Whoever abides in me and I in him, he it is that bears much fruit, for apart from me you can do nothing. If anyone does not abide in me he is thrown away like a branch and withers; and the branches are gathered, thrown into the fire, and burned. If you abide in me, and my words abide in you, ask whatever you wish, and it will be done for you. By this my Father is glorified, that you bear much fruit and so prove to be my disciples.

As the Father has loved me, so have I loved you. Abide in my love. If you keep my commandments, you will abide in my love, just as I have kept my Father's commandments and abide in his love. These things I have spoken to you, that my joy may be in you, and that your joy may be full.

This is my commandment, that you love one another as I have loved you. Greater love has no one than this, that someone lay down his life for his friends. You are my friends if you do what I command you. No longer do I call you servants, for the servant does not know what his master is doing; but I have called you friends, for all that I have heard from my Father I have made known to you. You did not choose me, but I chose you and appointed you that you should go and bear fruit and that your fruit should abide, so that whatever you ask the Father in my name, he may give it to you. These things I command you, so that you will love one another."

———

If you asked me where I live, I'd give you my home address. We don't use the word *dwell* very often, but my home is where I dwell. Or abide. Which is the word Jesus used multiple times in our passage. The Greek word is *menō*, and it is most often translated as "abide," but it can also be translated as "remain," "dwell," "continue," or "stay." It means to continue to be present in a place, to remain and continue to remain. This is what it means to abide.

1. How many times does Jesus use the word *abide*? Circle each one.

   List all the places you are to abide.

   _____

   _____

   Where does Jesus abide?

   _____

   _____

What is supposed to abide in you?

_____

_____

2. Regardless of your artistic ability, draw a picture that illustrates what Jesus is saying in verses 1–6.

3. Who is the vinedresser? What does he do to the branches that abide and bear fruit and to the branches that don't?

_____

_____

_____

_____

I'm not much of a gardener, but I do know that anything on my plants that is dead or diseased must be cut off. I prune the branches that grow the wrong way. I remove the dead flowers. I trim anything that keeps the plant from healthy growth and flourishing. If a branch could talk, I'm sure it would ask me why I was hurting it. I would explain, "I'm doing this so you will be stronger, better, and more fruitful." If I do this for plants that I hardly care about, how much more will God prune and care for us! Of course, he wants to remove, clip, cut off, and prune anything that will hinder our good growth. Of course, at times, his pruning is painful. But the good vinedresser is always caring for his own with great love and care. We can trust him to know what needs to be pruned.

4. What is the comparison Jesus makes in verse 9? What is the order of love and abiding?

_____

_____

_____

_____

5. What is the result for the person who abides in the love of Jesus and keeps his commandments?

_____

_____

_____

_____

6. Underline every phrase about bearing fruit. Who bears fruit? How?

_____

_____

_____

_____

7. After observing the text, what questions do you still have?

_____

_____

_____

_____

Abiding in Jesus—remaining, dwelling, and continuing to stay—is vital for the flourishing of all who follow Jesus. It is the way of abundant life. We will learn more this week about how we abide in Jesus, but, as you work on your memory verse, draw near to Jesus—he is the true source of everything you will ever need.

💜 **Memory Verse**

"I am the vine; you are the branches. Whoever abides in me and I in him, he it is that bears much fruit, for apart from me you can do nothing." *John 15:5*

INTERPRETATION
What Does the Text Mean?

I'm not a fan of receiving flowers as a gift. Never have been. Oh, they're beautiful—for a while. But as those beautiful flowers sit in a vase, they slowly decay. They drop their leaves and petals. The water grows moldy. And they're a mess to carry out to the trash. All of which I know is going to happen when the beautiful bouquet first arrives. Why? Because the flowers have been cut off from the vine that sustained, nourished, and gave them strength. They are dead, even though for a while, they appear to be alive. I don't want to be like a cut flower. And the only way to remain spiritually alive is if I am vitally connected to the true vine. That is what Jesus wanted his disciples, then and now, to know.

1. How do the different translations of *menō* (beginning of Day 1) help you better understand our English word *abide*? Write a short description of what it might mean to abide in Jesus.

2. Remembering that Jesus was talking to his disciples on the night before he was crucified, how might the timing of this passage inform the importance of abiding?

3. Describe the differences between a literal vine and a branch. How does that help us understand our metaphorical role as a branch?

4. How does the first half of verse 7 inform the second half? Similarly, how does the phrase "so that" in verse 16 help us understand what comes immediately after it?

I first put my trust in Jesus because of John 15:7b. I was in middle school and heard a youth pastor talk about how we could ask whatever we wished, and it would be given to us. I have no idea what he said about that verse, but the verse itself sounded pretty good to me. And if you just look at the second half of the verse—"Ask whatever you wish, and it will be done for you"—you might be like me and think that this sounds like a pretty good deal. The problem, though, is that as you walk with Jesus, you'll realize that you don't get everything you ask for. When that happens, one of two things will occur. You will either start to believe that the Bible is not true—or you will dive deeper into the Bible and let your understanding grow and change. Let's be women who do the latter.

5. What do you think Jesus meant by each phrase when he said that he "chose you and appointed you that you should go and bear fruit and that your fruit should abide" (v. 16)?

6. If the branch of a grapevine is cut off from the main vine, it quickly dries, crumbles, and turns into dust that blows away. How does that help us understand what Jesus said in verse 5, "Apart from me you can do nothing"? What do you think "do nothing" means?

7. In verses 9–11 Jesus said that he kept his Father's commandments and re-mained in his love, and that his joy was complete. What are the connections between obedience, abiding, bearing fruit, and joy?

_____

_____

_____

_____

It is important to note that bearing fruit is the *result* of abiding in the love of God, not how we earn the love of God. In other words, the fruit in our lives is not what makes us a disciple of Jesus; it is evidence that we are his disciple. As you work on your memory verse, rest knowing that the love of God is fixed and steady. Abide in it.

💜 Memory Verse

"I am the vine; you are the branches. Whoever abides in me and I in him, he it is that bears much fruit, for apart from me you can do nothing." *John 15:5*

INTERPRETATION
What Does the Whole Bible Say?

We haven't talked about it yet, but did you wonder why Jesus said that he is the *true* vine? By implication that means there is a false vine. His disciples would have known exactly what he meant because throughout the Old Testament, God refers to Israel as his vine.

1. Read Psalm 80:7–11. Where was the vine before God planted it? What did God have to do before he planted it? If you are familiar with the Old Testament, what events do you think the psalmist is referencing?

2. Many years after the psalmist wrote Psalm 80, the prophet Isaiah wrote to Israel. Read Isaiah 5:1–7. According to verse 7, who is the vineyard?

List everything the Lord did for his vineyard.

According to verse 4, what did the Lord expect from his vineyard?

According to verse 7, what was the Lord looking for and what did he find instead?

Israel was supposed to be fruitful. God saved them, delivered them, established them, and spoke to them. God blessed them to bless those around them and glorify God (Gen. 12:2). They were meant to abide in the good love of God. But they didn't do any of these things faithfully. They were not a faithful vine even though they had a faithful vinedresser.

Jesus came to be and fulfill everything God had spoken about Israel. The Father brought him out of Egypt (Matt. 2:13–15). He kept the Father's commandments. He brought the Father glory and abided in his love. Jesus embodied righteousness and justice. These things confirm that Jesus is the true vine promised in the Old Testament.

3. Read Ezekiel 15:1–8. How is this description of the vine different from the description Jesus gave in our passage this week? How does it help us better understand what good news it would have been to hear Jesus's words in John 15?

It's hard to read this passage without asking who the branches that are taken away and thrown into the fire represent. In other words, are they true believers? Can a true believer in Jesus lose her salvation? Can someone be a branch and then get cut off? If this were the only passage we had to answer that question, we might wonder. But we have the whole counsel of God's word (which is why we look to other passages in Scripture on Day 3), and we know that God's word never contradicts itself. The rule is that we let the clearer passages interpret the harder ones.

4. Go back and read John 6:37–39, a passage we studied in week 1. How secure is the person who comes to Jesus in faith?

5. Read John 10:28-29. What does Jesus say that no one will be able to do? What does Jesus say about perishing?

_____

_____

_____

_____

If anyone comes to Jesus in faith, that person will _never_ perish, _never_ be taken out of Jesus's hand, and _will be_ raised up on the last day. In other words, a Christian can never lose her salvation. Ever. So who are the branches that are taken away and burned?

The sad reality is that not everyone who _says_ she is a Christian is truly trusting in Christ. Lots of people go to church or say spiritual things, but in their hearts, they aren't really relying on Christ alone to save them. Those people may think they are Christians because they were baptized, or because their parents and grandparents were Christians, or because they are good and moral people. But none of these things make a person a Christian. The branches that are cut off and thrown away represent anyone who would anchor her salvation in something other than Christ.

A person becomes a Christian only by God's grace and through faith in Jesus. Only when a person recognizes that she is a sinner and can do nothing to earn her salvation—not by good works, not by being a good-enough person, or not by going to church—and turns to Jesus as her only hope will she become a true follower of Jesus. Only then will she never perish or be cut off. Our hope isn't in the strength of our faith. We will all have days and seasons where we feel weak or doubt. Our hope is in the finished work of the one who is always strong. He is the source of true salvation. Placing our faith in him is the way to be a true branch anchored in the true vine. And branches prove to be true branches by bearing fruit.

6. Read Galatians 5:22–23. List the fruit produced in a true follower of Jesus. How is it produced?

_____

_____

_____

_____

7. Read Ephesians 2:8–10. What role do good works play in salvation? What role do good works play in the life of a believer after salvation?

_____

_____

_____

_____

Oh, friend, if you have not come to Jesus in true faith, I urge you to let the words of this passage be a strong warning. But if you have come to Jesus in true faith, then rest assured you will never be taken away. You will be pruned, but not cut off. Abide and bear fruit. This is to our Father's glory.

💜 Memory Verse

"I am the vine; you are the branches. Whoever abides in me and I in him, he it is that bears much fruit, for apart from me you can do nothing." _John 15:5_

APPLICATION: *How Do I Faithfully Respond?* The Thursday night when the words of our passage were spoken had to be a very disorienting and frightening time for the disciples. They had grown accustomed to Jesus walking right next to them. They were used to being able to lean over and ask him questions. His presence in their midst had caused them to be strong and courageous. But now that he was preparing them for his departure, they were unsure of what the future would hold. I imagine that his command to abide in him was received with great relief and enthusiasm—*Yes, Jesus, I will abide, but how*? His answer to them is the same one that we need to hear—*Let my words abide in you.*

1. How do you let the word of God abide in you? How might the different translations of *menō* shed any light on your answer? What further insight does verse 10 offer?

2. What benefits do you see in this passage for the person who abides in the true vine? Do you see those benefits in your life? If so, describe.

3. Make a list of things the world might consider to be evidence of a fruitful life. How does this compare with the fruit the Bible speaks of? Which do you pursue most?

4. Are you a branch that bears fruit? How do you know? According to our passage, how important is bearing fruit in the life of a believer? How important is it to you that you bear fruit, much fruit, and fruit that will last?

5. Think about a fruit tree. Who does the fruit benefit? What should we expect about the fruit in our lives? Is it for us or for others?

6. Jesus said that his Father, the vinedresser, would prune fruitful branches. How have you been pruned, and what fruit did you see in your life as a result?

7. How did this passage change or enlarge the way you think about prayer?

8. How did this text help you see, believe, and live?

What did you see or learn about Jesus?

What do you need to believe as a result?

How should you live in response?

As we've beheld who Jesus is—the bread of life; the light of the world; the door; the good shepherd; the resurrection and the life; the way, the truth, and the life; and the true vine—my hope for all of us is that our belief has soared. I hope some of you came to true faith for the first time! We are praying for you. We also pray that those of you who have walked in faith for years have beheld Jesus in new and glorious ways. May our eyes be lifted to see more of him and our hearts be enlarged to love Jesus more today than we did yesterday. Until that glorious day when we will all see him face-to-face, may we abide in him.

🩶 Memory Verse

"I am the vine; you are the branches. Whoever abides in me and I in him, he it is that bears much fruit, for apart from me you can do nothing." *John 15:5*

REFLECTION

We used to live on 15 acres in Kansas. As is true in most of Kansas, there weren't many trees on our property, but there were rows of trees that lined the borders. If you've spent any time in Kansas, you know that the wind can blow fiercely! Part of the reason is that there aren't many trees to slow it down. After every storm, branches that had been blown off the trees were strewn across our property. My sons learned to drive their father's pickup truck long before they were old enough to drive on the road because my husband would send them around the pastures to pick up all the branches on the ground.

For every branch blown off, there were four times as many branches that remained on the trees. I always wondered what made the difference for the branch. Why were some blown off when the wind was strong, and some weren't? What made the connection between the branch and the trunk strong enough to withstand the storm?

Those branches on the ground make me think not only of our passage this week, but also of Jesus's words in Matthew 7:

> Everyone then who hears these words of mine and does them will be like a wise man who built his house on the rock. And the rain fell, and the floods came, and the winds blew and beat on that house, but it did not fall, because it had been founded on the rock. And everyone who hears these words of mine and does not do them will be like a foolish man who built his house on the sand. And the rain fell, and the floods came, and the winds blew and beat against that house, and it fell, and great was the fall of it. (Matt 7:24–27)

In the parable, both men built a house and both men faced storms. But one house stood in the face of the fierce winds, and one fell.

Jesus explained the parable as he taught it, and the astounding part is the difference between the two men. We might think the difference would be that one man heard the word of God and one didn't, but we read that both men heard the word of God. The difference was that the wise man *did the words* and the unwise man did not *do the words*. In other words, one man obeyed and kept the words of God, and one didn't.

Hearing the word of God is obviously not enough to keep your house, or mine, from falling. We have to be women who *do* the word of God—women who obey the word of God. In the same way that it's not enough to just go to church and be around "churchy" things, we have to not only hear the word of God but do it (James 1:22). That is how we will build houses that will not, that cannot, fall. And that is how we are branches that will not, that cannot, be cut off. It's not that our obedience earns our salvation, but it does prove our salvation is real.

Obedience is not a super popular word in our culture today. *Abiding* is much more inviting. It makes us feel all warm and fuzzy inside. And it should. It's a beautiful word that connotes love, relationship, life, and joy. But what we saw in our passage this week is that we cannot abide without obeying.

Obedience to God has always been required of God's children. In the garden of Eden, God required one thing from Adam and Eve—obey his one prohibition. Obedience to God's word mattered for all of God's people. He told Israel through Moses:

See, I am setting before you today a blessing and a curse: the blessing, if you obey the commandments of the LORD your God, which I command you today, and the curse, if you do not obey the commandments of the LORD your God, but turn aside from the way that I am commanding you today, to go after other gods that you have not known. (Deut. 11:26–28)

We don't obey to earn the love of God; we obey because we believe his ways are better and more trustworthy than our own. When we know and obey the word of God, we are so tightly tethered to him, the true vine, that we can rest secure. The winds and storms of life will come. But the true vine is a strong and mighty fortress. He will never be shaken or moved. Tether your life to his. Behold him. Believe him. Obey him. Abide in him. And you will live.

1. How does the parable in Matthew 7 shed light on the metaphor of the vine and the branches?

2. Why do you think that obeying God's word strengthens you for the storms of life?

💜 **Memory Verse**

"I am the vine; you are the branches. Whoever abides in me and I in him, he it is that bears much fruit, for apart from me you can do nothing." *John 15:5*

DISCUSSION QUESTIONS

Icebreaker: What is your favorite fruit?

Warm-up: Which of the fruit of the Spirit listed in Galatians 5 (love, joy, peace, patience, kindness, goodness, faithfulness, gentleness, and self-control) do you want to see more of in your life?

1. What is the result for the person who abides in the love of Jesus and keeps his commandments? What do you think this looks like in our lives?

_____

_____

_____

_____

2. How do the different translations of *menō* (beginning of Day 1) help you better understand our English word *abide*?

_____

_____

_____

_____

3. In verses 9–11 Jesus said that he kept his Father's commandments and remained in his love, and that his joy was complete. What are the connections between obedience, abiding, bearing fruit, and joy?

4. Read Ephesians 2:8–10. What role do good works play in salvation? What role do good works play in the life of a believer after salvation?

5. Jesus said that his Father, the vinedresser, would prune fruitful branches. In what ways have you been pruned, and what fruit did you see in your life as a result?

6. How did this passage change or enlarge the way you think about prayer?

7. How did this text help you see, believe, and live?

What did you see or learn about Jesus?

What do you need to believe as a result?

How should you live differently?

8. What was one thing that stood out/convicted/encouraged/instructed you this week?

TGC | THE GOSPEL COALITION

The Gospel Coalition (TGC) supports the church in making disciples of all nations, by providing gospel-centered resources that are trusted and timely, winsome and wise.

Guided by a Council of more than 40 pastors in the Reformed tradition, TGC seeks to advance gospel-centered ministry for the next generation by producing content (including articles, podcasts, videos, courses, and books) and convening leaders (including conferences, virtual events, training, and regional chapters).

In all of this we want to help Christians around the world better grasp the gospel of Jesus Christ and apply it to all of life in the 21st century. We want to offer biblical truth in an era of great confusion. We want to offer gospel-centered hope for the searching.

Through its women's initiatives, the Gospel Coalition aims to support the growth of women in faithfully studying and sharing the Scriptures; in actively loving and serving the church; and in spreading the gospel of Jesus Christ in all their callings.

Join us by visiting TGC.org so you can be equipped to love God with all your heart, soul, mind, and strength, and to love your neighbor as yourself.

TGC.org

Also Available from the Gospel Coalition

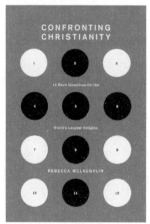

For more information, visit **crossway.org**.